D0772289

# KING DAVID

# KING DAVID

### LESSONS ON LEADERSHIP
### FROM THE LIFE OF DAVID

## TOM HOUSTON

A ministry of World Vision

MARC
EUROPE

**British Library Cataloguing in Publication Data**

Houston, Tom, *1928–*
   King David.
   1. David, *King of Israel*
   I. Title
   221.9′24     BS580.D3

   ISBN 0–947697–59–4

Unless otherwise stated, all Scripture quotations are from the Good News Bible, © American Bible Society 1966, 1971, 1976, published by The Bible Societies and Collins, and are used by permission.

Cover picture: David receiving water from the well at Bethlehem from the hands of Abishai. (Stained glass, Musée de Strasbourg.)

MARC Europe is an integral part of World Vision, an international Christian humanitarian organisation. MARC's object is to assist Christian leaders with factual information surveys, management skills, strategic planning and other tools for evangelism. MARC Europe also publishes and distributes related books on matters of mission, church growth, management, spiritual maturity and other topics.

# Dedication

To all my friends, the *wananchi* of Kenya, who by their courage and example, their friendship and patience, their achievements and their unmet needs drove me deeper into the Bible, to find its message much more relevant than I ever would have discovered it otherwise.

# Acknowledgements

I am indebted to the congregation of Nairobi Baptist Church for giving me the opportunity and the encouragement to work on this material. Many authors and commentators have fed me with their insights, and some provoked me with their dullness to my own original thoughts. James Gibson has been responsible for producing the written manuscript from my notes and spoken text, and I am extremely grateful to him. Nathan Showalter, my assistant, has prodded and encouraged me to keep the work moving. The staff of MARC Europe have been consistently helpful and diligent—I am grateful to them all.

# Contents

# Introduction

David has fascinated me since I was a boy. My real work on my hero was, however, done in Nairobi between 1967 and 1969, about five years after Kenya became independent and while she was still struggling to shape her nationhood. The chapters of this book were originally delivered as sermons in that very dynamic context. One of them was given on Kenyatta Day in October, when Kenya remembers those who died in her struggle for freedom. Chapter XIII, 'Rivalry and Revenge', was preached on July 6th, 1969, less than 24 hours after Tom Mboya was assassinated, and while his body still lay about 200 yards away in the mortuary. Chapter X, 'Self-interest', where David and his men behave like mercenaries, was broadcast at the end of a week when mercenaries in the Congo were every day in the newspaper headlines. Several of the sermons were broadcast live when we knew that President Kenyatta or his ministers might well be listening. Having such an audience forced me to think clearly and to apply Scripture to the African context even before contextualising had become the vogue.

I spoke with Paul's conviction about the Old Testament. 'All these things happened to them as examples for others, and they were written down as a warning for us. For we live at a time when the end is about to come' (I Cor 10:11). I drew what I could from the commentaries and earlier writers on David such as F B Meyer, Alan Redpath, and John Hercus. From these I benefitted greatly but found I needed something more. I was not looking to see how David became a 'man of God'; I was more interested in how he learned to lead a people from its tribal period to nationhood. For this there was little help in the commentaries. The histories of the Old Testament were of more help, but most of the basic work on the text had to be my own, in the light of the vivid and changing context in which we were living in Kenya. The attempt was practical rather than scholarly.

In the preparation of these sermons now for presentation to a wider audience both in the Third World and in the West, I have made significant revisions. I have tried to make the chapters readable and have moved away from the idiom of the spoken word. There is loss in this. The didactic application is muted, and readers who are preachers will have to work harder to extract the sermon points. Repetition—a necessity in preaching—has largely been eliminated, not only within chapters, but between one chapter and another. This cuts out almost all background matter, which will now be found in earlier chapters.

The natural movement from the Old Testament to the New in preaching has been acknowledged by the addition of an appropriate statement of Jesus or the Apostles on the page facing the beginning of each chapter. The paragraphs which in the original sermons made that transition have been regretfully omitted.

So far as the student is concerned, this book should drive him or her back to the biblical text to 'prove all things' and only 'hold fast that which is good'. That is the responsibility of all Christian audiences and readers and the test of all preachers and writers.

I send out this little volume with a prayer that it may teach you, as it has me, something about leadership in your own sphere of life.

*Tom Houston*

**The heart is the man.**

*Whoever is faithful in small matters will be faithful in large ones.*

— Luke 16:10

# I
# Getting Started
*I Samuel 16*

### Times Were Bad

David grew up in an unstable political climate. Saul, Israel's first head of state, had a promising start to his reign, but power went to his head. He interfered in religious affairs and ended up by having a head-on clash with his mentor, the prophet Samuel. This was a deep disappointment to the older man, who had been instrumental in selecting Saul when the new regime was instituted by popular demand. Things came to a head when Saul took the line of least resistance and greatest personal advantage in dealing with the neighbouring Amalekite people. The old prophet broke with the king and told him he had forfeited God's help and protection.

Not long after that, Samuel was ordered to Bethlehem to pick a successor to Saul from the household of one of the leading families.

### The Secret Sacrifice

Broad-shouldered, tall, handsome, they passed one by one in front of Samuel as the strong smell of the burning sacrifice filled the air. 'This man ... is surely the one God has chosen,' thought Samuel as he saw Jesse's oldest son Eliab approach the heifer on the stone altar. Muscles rippled under Eliab's tunic; he gave a confident smile to Samuel, who stood ready to anoint the next king over Israel. Even as Samuel tightened his grip on the horn of oil, however, the voice of God stopped him. 'Pay no attention to how tall and handsome he is ... Man looks at the outward appearance, but I look at the heart' (verses 6–7). Samuel motioned Eliab to move on. Surprised, perhaps somewhat piqued, he passed by the altar, and Jesse called Abinadab. 'No, the Lord hasn't chosen him either.' Abinadab passed by the altar and Jesse called Shammah. 'No, the Lord hasn't chosen him either.' Shammah passed by the altar, and Jesse called his remaining sons. 'No, the Lord hasn't chosen any of these' (verses 8–10). With ritual regularity the refrain sounded, as one by one Jesse's sons passed unchosen in front of Samuel.

'Have you any more sons?' asked Samuel tersely. Jesse mentioned David, hardly worth bothering about, since he was just a boy tending the sheep. But Samuel cut him short with a peremptory command: 'Tell him to come here. We won't offer the sacrifice until he comes' (verse 11). The seven sons of Jesse exchanged quizzical glances; impatience rose in Eliab's face, but only the sound of sizzling fat from the roasting heifer dropping on the hot stones broke the silence as Samuel awaited the approach of David.

There were good reasons both for silence and for speed in this secret ceremony. Behind his impassive exterior the prophet Samuel hid his dread of Saul and his fear that news of this visit to Bethlehem would reach Saul's ears. Saul had not turned out right. He had mismanaged the affairs of state. Ever since his fateful clash with Saul, Samuel had gone into voluntary retirement at Ramah. Now, aged and respected though he was, he feared for his life. When the Lord told him to anoint a new king to replace Saul, Samuel had said, 'How can I do that? If Saul hears about it, he will kill me!' (verse 2). A trip from Ramah to Bethlehem would look suspicious at best and court danger at worst. People lived in a state of uncertainty; city leaders fearfully watched for trouble. When Samuel finally embarked on his secret mission to Bethlehem, the city leaders came trembling to meet him and asked, 'Is this a peaceful visit?' (verse 4). Under the pretext of offering a ritual sacrifice with the people of Bethlehem, Samuel had called the sons of Jesse before him one by one, and now he waited beside the sacrifice for the final son to appear.

Then David stood there before the altar, with a ruddy complexion and handsome features like the rest, skilled at the harp, well-spoken, as yet untested in battle but brave like his brothers. Immediately the Lord said to Samuel, 'This is the one—anoint him!' (verse 13). And as the oil dripped from David's hair to the ground, his long career in leadership began.

## Heredity and Character

Why did God choose David over his brothers? As the seven sons of Jesse passed before Samuel, their height and fine appearance masked the tangled and complicated family relationships which had formed their characters. Jesse belonged to the high-ranking clan of the Ephrathites in the tribe of Judah. His great-grandfather Boaz, the wealthy landowner, had married Ruth. With his first wife Jesse had raised a family of seven sons, at least three of whom had followed Saul into the army. Late in his life Jesse had married again either the widow or the concubine of Nahash, King of the Ammonites, who had brought with her two remarkable daughters, Zeruiah and Abigail. Of this second union David was born and grew up with Abishai and Joab, the sons of his step-sister Zeruiah.

Sent to the fields to herd the sheep, David seems to have received little attention from his father, who had to be reminded of his existence by Samuel at the sacrifice. Nor did his older brothers treat him with much kindness or appreciation. There is evidence of a long-established pattern of sibling rivalry, jealousy, and recrimination. Depth psychologists could have had a field day with this young man.

With an aged father who paid him little attention, seven older step-brothers who disliked him, and two enterprising older step-sisters and their families to contend with, David could have become an aggressive delinquent with a constant chip on his shoulder, used to fighting for whatever he could get and defiant of authority. But he did not because his heart was right. Samuel had told Saul earlier that the Lord would 'find the kind of man he wants' (I Sam 13:14).

Now Samuel had found him in the most unlikely circumstances—not in the equivalent in that day of a happy nuclear family with two healthy, well-adjusted children attending the right schools and living in the best neighbourhood. He was the youngest in a widely extended family of children of different mothers, an aged father and all the domestic infighting that goes with that. In spite of his family background, David's heart was right and he did his shepherd tasks with diligence and courage and grew to be the man God chose to be king over Israel.


### The First Assignment

We do not know what, if anything, Samuel said that day

when he poured the oil over David's head. Josephus says
that Samuel told David the significance of the ceremony,
and if Josephus is correct, such intimations of greatness
could easily have turned the head of Israel's future leader.
But the Spirit of the Lord took control of David and was
with him from that day on. He returned to herding his
father's sheep and carrying messages to his stepbrothers in
Saul's army. He must have wondered as he sat watching the
sheep graze what the next step would be, but he was learning that the Lord was his shepherd and trusted that he
would lead him.

'Send me your son David, the one who takes care of the
sheep' (I Sam 16:19). When the message came from Saul's
court at Gibeah, David must have been elated, but not surprised. Finally it was happening. The anointed king of
Israel had been summoned to the palace. After all, it made
sense. What could be more logical?

Imagine, then, his dismay when he learned that he had
been summoned not to some great task, but to carry the
King's armour and to play his harp when Saul suffered from
depression and melancholy. He was to be a common servant—a minstrel. How far from what he had thought as the
oil trickled down his brow during that secret sacrifice in
Bethlehem! Yet because his heart was right, he looked on it
as an opportunity, did his duty well and learned from it. No
other king in Israel before him had grown up in the palace.
The only previous experience Saul had had was looking
after his father's asses. He had known nothing about court
procedure and protocol, about palace intrigue and power.
Like Moses, who had grown up in the court of Pharaoh and
went on to lead his people, David was receiving his intro-
duction to leadership. As he played music for Saul, he
studied him, observing his moods and lifting his spirits and
learning the power of music. He watched the ambassadors

and messengers from foreign countries and learned about the affairs of state. He served his apprenticeship faithfully, playing his instrument to the limit of his powers, keeping his eyes and ears open, and trusting God to take care of the rest.

**Build on what you know.**

*If you have faith as big as a mustard seed … you could do anything.*

— Jesus in Matthew 17:20

# II
# The Signs of Developing Leadership
*I Samuel 17*

### A Bombastic Leader

'Choose one of your men to fight me!' shouted Goliath. 'If he wins and kills me, we will be your slaves; but if I win and kill him, you will be our slaves. Here and now I challenge the Israelite army' (verses 8–10).

The thundering challenge of Goliath dismayed and terrified Saul and his army. For six weeks Goliath had battered the Israelites with his challenge, and for six weeks the ranks of Saul's army had fled in great fear from their battle positions.

Small wonder! Goliath stood over nine feet tall, bronze helmet on his head, bronze greaves on his legs, a bronze coat of armour weighing 125 pounds protecting his body, and a bronze javelin slung on his back. His spear shaft looked like the barana weaver's loom and the iron point alone weighed 15 pounds. Unassailed and unchallenged, champion of the Philistines, Goliath towered above the Philistine rank and file at his back and intimidated the Israelites in his path.

How did Goliath become a leader? Given modern medical

science, we might postulate because of hyperactivity in his pituitary glands during adolescence his longitudinal bone growth had continued long beyond its normal cessation. Due to this genetic accident he had aggressively challenged, fought, and won his way to the top. Everything rested on his greater reach with a sword and his longer throw with the spear. With bravado and bombast he had hypnotised the Israelites and the Philistines into believing that the outcome of the battle depended on his physical size and strength alone. Mesmerised by his performance, both armies forgot about what really wins battles—tactics and strategy, the logistics of terrain and weaponry, the morale, fitness, and number of their soldiers.

Behind the bravado and bombast, however, David saw the fragile strength of Goliath's leadership. The clanking of the bronze armour, the rippling muscles of his bare arms and the taunting challenge impressed and awed the opposition, but Goliath and the Philistines had all their strength in one area to the neglect of the others. When David called Goliath's bluff and fought him with sling and stone instead of sword and spear, Goliath's advantage disappeared. Stunned by the stone, he crashed to the ground, the shattered fragments of his bombast lying in pieces around him.

## A Demoralised Leader

Why didn't Saul see through Goliath's façade as David did? In the dialogue of the story Saul speaks only twice, and his first speech shows him to be completely demoralised: 'How could you fight him? You're just a boy and he has been a soldier all his life!' (verse 33). Like his men, Saul had been hypnotised by Goliath's lie. He could think only in terms of physical strength and prowess in battle, and no one he knew had the sheer size or strength or courage to match Goliath. His resourcefulness disappeared.

It had not always been like that. After Saul had become king over Israel, he had gone out against his enemies everywhere. He had fought heroically and victoriously everywhere, and had delivered Israel from all attacks (I Sam 14:47–48). Now, when the Philistines threatened Israel, however, he couldn't muster the old heroism and courage.

In the beginning Saul had drawn his confidence and ability from God, but from the moment he came to power he stopped listening to anyone. He cut himself off from the wise political advice and spiritual counsel of Samuel. He had started out humble but had ended up arrogant (I Sam 15:23). He overstepped himself, and took on tasks that belonged to other men. Material possessions became too important to him and interfered with his judgement. He began to rationalise his mistakes and make excuses for his blunders (15:9–21).

When he finally realised what was happening his only concern was to save face. Catching hold of Samuel's robe and falling to his knees, he begged, 'At least show me respect in front of the leaders of my people and all Israel' (15:30). Samuel did, but Saul ended up with only the trappings of power. Nothing remained except the empty shell. Now suffering from deep depression, violent temper, and incurable envy, he was demoralised before Goliath, powerless to lead his army to victory.

## A Budding Leader

David was marked out from everyone else that day by refusing to be deceived about the real issue: 'Who is this

heathen Philistine to defy the armies of the living God?'
(I Sam 17:26). Presented with the boastful posturing of
Goliath and the demoralisation of Saul's army, he saw
where the real issue lay. The real problem was not in the objective conditions created by the size of one man, but in the
subjective conditions that existed in the attitudes of the
Israelites. They had lost faith in the promises that God had
given to them. That was the real trouble. David saw the
same scene as everyone else did, but saw it differently. He
refused to be hypnotised by the popular view and penetrated to the one important factor that could be changed
and that would change everything else.

David also applied practical wisdom derived from previous experience:

> I take care of my father's sheep. Whenever a lion or a
> bear carries off a lamb, I go after it, attack it, and res-
> cue the lamb. And if the lion or bear turns on me, I
> grab it by the throat and beat it to death. I have killed
> lions and bears, and I will do the same to this heathen
> Philistine, who has defied the army of the living God.
> The Lord has saved me from lions and bears; he will
> save me from this Philistine.
>
> (I Sam 17:34–37)

Experience does not by itself produce wisdom or ensure
success, but experience interpreted accurately does. David
recalled his own previous experience of fear and danger
and God's protection, and he projected accurately the lines
of known past experience into a new situation in the faith
that God remains the same even if conditions change. If
God protected him against lions and bears, he would also
protect him against Goliath. If God helped him to save his
flock, he would also help him to save his nation as long as he
was doing what God wanted him to do. 'Give yourself to

the Lord,' David wrote later; 'trust in him, and he will help you; he will make your righteousness shine like the noonday sun' (Ps 37:5–6).

In choosing to defy Goliath and to trust in God's protection, David was not simply tackling the spectacular or tempting providence. He was not accustomed to fighting unnecessary battles. His objective was not to kill lions; it was to save sheep. He was not a hunter but a shepherd. He concentrated on protecting the sheep, not on building his own ego by slaying predators. When he accepted Goliath's challenge, David was motivated not by the wealth, freedom from taxation and marriage to the king's daughter promised by Saul, but by his desire to defend God's honour: 'This very day ... I will give the bodies of the Philistine soldiers to the birds and animals to eat. Then the whole world will know that Israel has a God' (I Sam 17:46).

David also had the courage that Saul lacked to think independently. He was not encouraged in this action. Everyone, even King Saul, advised against what he proposed (verse 33). He had to back his own judgement. He had to ignore the opinions of lesser men and the taunts of his eldest brother, who questioned his motives and accused him of deserting his sheep to watch the excitement of the battle (verse 28).

When Saul saw that David was determined to fight Goliath, he tried to tell him how to do it. He dressed David in a bronze helmet and a coat of armour and even gave David his own sword—a princely gift indeed, since at one point Saul and Jonathan had the only swords in the entire Israelite army. The Philistines held a monopoly on the iron trade and saw to it that no swords or spears were manufactured for Israel (I Sam 13:19–22). But David rejected this well-intentioned help. He insisted on staying within the field of his proven experience and competence. He shed Saul's heavy armour and armed himself only with his sling and stones.

He was not without resourcefulness, however, even where he was inexperienced. After stunning Goliath with the stone, David used a sword, Goliath's own sword, to kill him and cut off his head. Later he added the sword to his own armoury.

It was a significant day for David. It brought him to public attention in a big way, but more significantly it showed in him qualities that were to be projected much further in future. It gave him more experience to convert into wisdom, and further strengthened his greatest assets—his faith in God and his desire to honour him.

**Appoint under you better people than yourself.**

*They are envious ... I warn you ... these who do those things will not possess the Kingdom of God.*

— Paul in Galatians 5:21

# III
# Envy
*I Samuel chapters 18–20*

'The Lord has torn the kingdom of Israel away from you today and given it to someone who is a better man than you' (I Sam 15:28). Long before the defeat of Goliath Samuel had foreseen the fatal dynamics of the developing drama between Saul and David. When he told Saul that day in Gilgal that God had rejected him as king over Israel, Samuel also clearly intimated that an abler man would soon appear as a rival contender for the throne. Now it had happened. David was the man.

### Saul's Rival

Even though he had acted quite naturally and innocently, David could hardly have made it worse for Saul if he had tried. His victory over Goliath galled the king. Saul belonged to the tribe of Benjamin, a tribe famous for its skill with the sling (Judg 20:15–16). Saul must have felt foolish after all his fuss in trying to get David to use his precious metal armour, only to watch David bring down Goliath with the very skill in which Benjaminites were supposed to excel. When he inquired whose son David was, and discovered that he came from Bethlehem of Judah, the tribe largest in numbers and richest in territory, it only made matters worse and stung like salt added to his battle wounds.

David's triumph over Goliath captured the imagination of the people, who went wild with delight over this young hero. Saul rewarded David with a high position in the army, and the officers and soldiers took the new commander to their hearts (I Sam 18:5). 'Everyone in Israel and Judah loved David, because he was such a successful leader' (18:16). When they returned from fighting the Philistines, the women came out of the towns and villages, singing and dancing to the sound of lutes and tambourines. 'Saul has killed thousands, but David tens of thousands' (18:7). Even Saul's own family started falling for the new hero. His son and heir to the throne, Jonathan, became David's bosom friend and swore a covenant of friendship with him (18:1–4). The princess, his daughter Michal, made matters worse by falling in love with David, and he soon found that he had David for a son-in-law as well as a rival (18:20–29). The old prophet Samuel, who had refused even to see Saul any more, protected David from Saul's messengers (I Sam 19:18–24).

Saul could only see the tapestry of his life's work unravelling. For centuries Israel had been a collection of tribes with no cohesion. At first Samuel, then Saul, had begun to weave them together, to create some unity, with leadership from Benjamin. God had been with Saul; now, however, God had rejected him, and he judged that David posed the threat of an alternative centre of power and popularity. Soon he would rival even Saul's position on the throne. Because he was a small man and getting smaller he could not see that together they could have united all Israel. Instead, by his jealousy he divided the nation and brought about its further defeat.

## Saul's Reaction

Saul's first reaction was anger when he heard the women's song: 'For David they claim tens of thousands, but only thousands for me. They will be making him king next!' (I Sam 18:8). Anger provoked suspicion, and Saul placed David under surveillance, jealously watching his movements. Every new report of David's success provided evidence that God was with David and had abandoned Saul, and Saul became afraid—afraid 'because the Lord was with David' (18:12), afraid because David was successful (18:15), afraid because his daughter loved David (18:29). Soon his obsessive fear turned to violence. Twice he personally tried to kill David with a spear in the palace while he played his harp. Only his fleetness of foot saved David as he dodged the missile and escaped even as Saul pulled the quivering spear from the wall to hurl it again (18:10–11; 19:9–10).

When it became obvious that he could not personally catch David off guard, Saul resorted to more sophisticated means to do away with him. Pretending to honour him but secretly hoping that he would be killed, Saul promoted David, made him a commander of a thousand men, and sent him on dangerous military missions. Instead, David's success in battle simply increased his popularity (18:13–14).

Saul persisted in his duplicity. Remembering his promise to marry his daughter to the man who killed Goliath, Saul offered David his oldest daughter Merab: '"Here is my elder daughter Merab. I will give her to you as your wife on condition that you serve me as a brave and loyal soldier, and fight the Lord's battles." (Saul was thinking that in this way the Philistines would kill David, and he would not have to do it himself)' (18:17). David's modest refusal foiled that scheme, but Saul tried again. When he

discovered that his daughter Michal was in love with
David, he was pleased. 'I'll give Michal to David; I will
use her to trap him, and he will be killed by the Philistines'
(18:21). This time he tried to ensure David's death by
asking a bride price of 100 Philistine foreskins. Un-
daunted, David undertook the bloody escapade, and, unscathed, he doubled the dowry, delivering to Saul 200
Philistine foreskins. Nothing seemed to touch David, and
Saul became even more afraid.

Nothing deterred Saul from his mad programme of assassination by proxy, not even his own children's happiness.
He had not scrupled to trade his daughters' happiness in
marriage as the price for David's death. Now he sent messengers to kill David in his bed and roundly condemned his
daughter for not co-operating in the plot and for allowing
David to escape (I Sam 19:11–17). And when Jonathan
would not betray David, obsessive rage possessed Saul and
he hurled his spear at his son and heir, trying to kill him just
as he had tried before to kill David (I Sam 20:33).

From anger to suspicion, from suspicion to fear, from
fear to violence, envy had transformed Saul and consumed
his leadership with obsessive jealousy of David. At the beginning of his reign he had been known for his ability to en-
list able men. Wherever he found a man who was strong or
brave, he would take him in his service (I Sam 14:52). At
the end of his reign he could not tolerate David's ability or
success anywhere near him. Ironically, his own regime
weakened by the day because of his preoccupation with his
rival. He could think only about David, constantly compar-
ing David's present success to his own past success. The
plots and schemes to secure his own position diverted Saul
from the business of leadership and prevented him from
doing anything constructive. Insecure in himself and no
longer depending on God, he could not tolerate a rival.

## David's Reaction

If Saul's life is a notable case study in envy, David's is even more remarkably a case study of how to handle envy. Amazingly, all through this period when Saul vented on David his venom and spite, David moved with complete equanimity and remained positive in his attitudes. He played his harp for Saul (I Sam 18:10) and he completed successfully every mission assigned to him (18:5); David did not let all his successes go to his head. When the suggestion of marriage to the king's daughter arose, his simplicity won through: 'Who am I and what is my family that I should become the king's son-in-law? ... It's a great honour ... too great for someone poor and insignificant like me' (18:18, 23).

How did David achieve such success and remain so positive in the face of Saul's envy? Like a refrain throughout the text comes the statement, 'The Lord was with him' (18:12, 14, 28). That was his secret. His future didn't depend on his own efforts. God would protect him. Whatever fame he won was God's gift. In the Psalms, David wrote:

> Don't be worried on account of the wicked;
>    don't be jealous of those who do wrong.
> They will soon disappear like grass that dries up;
>    they will die like plants that wither.
> Trust in the Lord and do good;
>    live in the land and be safe.
> Seek your happiness in the LORD,
>    and he will give you your heart's desire.
>
>                                    (Ps 37:1–4)

He handled Saul's envy, then, by ignoring it, by patiently trusting God, and by behaving quite naturally. The man who is eaten up with repaying evil for evil has no energy left for constructive work. If David had been sidetracked into countering Saul's envy, he would not have had the success that won his acceptance by the people and secured his fame. It is greatness in a leader when, like Saul in his early days, he can surround himself with people of talent and distinction and when, like David, envy cannot touch him. The secret of such equanimity is the knowledge that in the last analysis success is won neither by brain nor by brawn, but is given by God.

**Find a friend who will remain honest with you.**

*I call you friends because I have told you everything.*
— John 15:15

# IV
# Friendship
*I Samuel chapters 18–20*

David's equanimity in the face of Saul's vindictive and irrational envy needs further explanation, but the secret is not hard to find. When Charles Kingsley was once asked about the secret of his happy, buoyant spirit all through life, he answered, 'I had a friend.' David too had a friend: Jonathan. David and Jonathan—their names, a byword for lasting friendship, are inseparably linked wherever the Bible has been translated and read.

## The Forming of a Friendship

As Goliath toppled to the ground, the Israelites had surged forward with a shout, pursuing the Philistines to the gates of their walled city, killing those who fell by the way, and plundering the Philistine camp on their return. David contented himself with securing Goliath's weapons and head, and then, escorted by Abner, the commander of the army, reported to Saul. Waiting beside the king stood his son Jonathan. As the two listened to David, the same words that provoked Saul to envy another who was better than himself aroused in Jonathan a love for David as strong as his love for himself (I Sam 18:1).

Plato was to teach that at the creation all souls came from the Creator as twins. Separated by the imperfection of the world, each soul hungers and yearns and searches for its mate. Such an idea, though only a philosopher's fancy, almost seems confirmed in the case of David and Jonathan who when they discovered each other became 'one in spirit' (18:1, NIV) as David talked.

The two young men, standing out starkly from their mediocre backgrounds because of their unusual excellence, suddenly found in each other an ideal they had long hoped for, but never found. Jonathan, no mean soldier himself, had shown the same deep religious faith coupled with extraordinary daring that he had witnessed in David facing Goliath. In his case, accompanied only by his armourbearer, he had tackled a Philistine garrison on his own, killed 20 men, and routed the rest. 'Nothing can keep him [God] from giving us the victory, no matter how few of us there are' (I Sam 14:6) he said on that occasion, words that echoed David's confident faith as he faced Goliath: 'Everyone here will see that the Lord does not need swords or spears to save his people' (17:47).

Their faith and courage drew them together as naturally as sword and shield, sling and stone. Their prior commitment to God undergirded their commitment to each other. 'The Lord will make sure that we will keep it [our promise] for ever' (I Sam 20:23). When Jonathan found David, he found a friend whom he admired and determined never to let go.

Jonathan swore eternal friendship with tangible tokens. 'Jonathan took off the robe he was wearing and gave it to David, together with his armour and also his sword, bow and belt' (I Sam 18:4). These were the insignia of his status as the king's son, and his conferring them on David symbolised just how much he was prepared to be committed to his friend. The grasping envy and rivalry that so embittered his father against David just never arose in Jonathan. All that he was and all that he could do he placed at the disposal of his friend, for he loved him as he loved himself.

## The Demands of Friendship

As Jonathan soon discovered, it is a costly business to make a best friend. Friends often make promises they cannot keep, but best friends spontaneously and naturally can ask each other to do anything, confident that promises will be honoured and requests will not be denied.

Jonathan learned how costly love could be when Saul ordered him and his servants to kill David. Caught between obeying his father and protecting his friend, Jonathan first warned David, then confronted Saul. He argued that Saul had no evidence of David's disloyalty and insisted that David had acted consistently in Saul's and the country's interests. Attempting to call out such good as still remained in his father, he pleaded, 'Sir, don't do wrong to your servant David. He has never done you any wrong' (I Sam 19:4). His persuasion worked. Saul made a vow in the Lord's name that he would not kill David, and Jonathan brought David back to court.

The reconciliation, however, was short-lived. When war broke out again with the Philistines, David's new successes in battle deepened Saul's depression and renewed his envy. While David sat at table playing his harp, once again Saul tried to kill him with his spear. With the help of his wife Michal, David escaped to Samuel at Ramah and then met secretly again with Jonathan.

For a second time friendship made demands on

Jonathan, and this time the cost of friendship came dear. Brushing aside Jonathan's assurances of his safety, David swore an oath and insisted that Jonathan was deceived about his own father. Many friendships have folded for lesser reasons, but Jonathan's loyalty remained firm and open-ended: '"I'll do anything you want," he said' (I Sam 20:4). Jonathan agreed to offer excuses for David's absence from Saul's table in order to test Saul's anger, and when the anger flared up, Jonathan, not David, was burned: 'Now I know you are taking sides with David and are disgracing yourself and that mother of yours! Don't you realise that as long as David is alive, you will never be king of this country? Now go and bring him here—he must die!' (20:30–31). When Jonathan stubbornly continued to plead David's case, Saul in an irrational fit of anger hurled his spear at Jonathan, trying to kill his own son and heir. In risking even his life to defend his friend, Jonathan willingly paid the price of friendship. 'The greatest love a person can have for his friends,' Jesus once said, 'is to give his life for them' (John 15:13).

Perhaps the most beautiful feature of this great friendship was how small a part office or status or position played in the life of either man. Jonathan had first expressed it with his symbolic gift of royal robe and armour. In their secret meeting in the Desert of Ziph where David was hiding, Jonathan declared openly, 'You are the one who will be king of Israel and … I will be next in rank to you' (I Sam 23:17). In the end Jonathan's friendship with David cost him the throne, but for Jonathan, unlike Saul, the throne was never the issue.

Nor did the issue arise for David. He knew that he had been anointed king only because God had chosen him. He did not rush into office, nor did he fight Saul. What it cost David to remain loyal to Jonathan through years of hiding in desert caves, of living as a marked man on the run, forms the subject of the next chapters. Holding true to his oath after the death of Saul and Jonathan on Mount Gilboa, he did not oppose Jonathan's brother as long as he ruled in the North. After his own kingdom had been established, he even brought Jonathan's crippled son Mephibosheth to live at the palace and royally maintained him for the rest of his life—a symbol of his undying friendship even after Jonathan's death.

## The Benefits of Friendship

All men, and especially leaders, hide behind masks. For leaders there are masks of corporate responsibility, masks of company policy, masks of official silence. It takes a great leader to maintain a genuine human spirit behind the mask; it takes an even greater leader to set the mask aside. The Psalms show that David knew how to take off his mask.

Everyone needs at least one other person with whom he can be completely honest, with whom he can remove his mask. Is it too much to imagine that the one who taught David to take off his mask was Jonathan? Right to the end of his life, honesty and openness marked David. How much of David's humanity, humility, and honesty derived from Jonathan we can only guess. How much the memory of their friendship saved him from bitterness, revenge and harsh judgement we shall never know. We are left only with his lament to carry to our hearts the importance of genuinely open friendship in making men God-like and making leaders human:

How the mighty have fallen in battle! Jonathan lies slain on your heights. I grieve for you, Jonathan my brother; you were very dear to me. Your love for me was wonderful, more wonderful than that of women. How the mighty have fallen!

(II Sam 1:25–27, NIV)

**A lie has a short life,**
**But truth lives on for ever.**

— **Proverbs 12:19**

*Whoever wants to enjoy life and wishes to see good times*
*must keep from speaking evil and stop telling lies.*

— I Peter 3:10

# V
# Truth
*I Samuel chapters 20–22*

While he hid like an outlaw in the hills, David's friendship with Jonathan remained deep and his loyalty to Saul unwavering, and yet he struggled with moral questions that face everyone who has to lead. The first issue dogged him the moment he began to run: How truthful should he be? Is it right to lie when it seems necessary to save one's skin or one's cause?

## David's Reasons for Lying

Saul had twice tried to kill him as he played his harp in the court, but David had dodged the spear and escaped. Saul had ordered his soldiers to kill David as he slept, but Michal his wife had helped David to escape. Saul had sent soldiers to Ramah where David hid with Samuel, but three times God had protected him by sending Saul's soldiers into a prophetic trance, and David had escaped. Unsafe at court with the king's son, unsafe at home with the king's daughter, unsafe even with the prophet Samuel, David grasped for his last hope: a secret meeting with Jonathan. Jonathan's assurances of David's safety notwithstanding, David feared for his life, and out of that fear sprang his first lie.

Determined to know where he stood, he pushed his friend Jonathan into a compromising situation. He fabricated a story giving a false explanation of his absence from a festival and begged Jonathan to use it to test out his father:

> Tomorrow is the New Moon Festival ... and I am supposed to eat with the king. But if it's all right with you, I will go and hide in the fields until the evening of the day after tomorrow. If your father notices that I am not at table, tell him that I begged your permission to hurry home to Bethlehem, since it's the time of the annual sacrifice there for my whole family. If he says, 'All right,' I will be safe; but if he becomes angry, you will know that he is determined to harm me.
>
> (I Sam 20:5–7)

Jonathan consented, but Saul's anger drove a deeper wedge between him and his father and nearly resulted in Saul's killing his own son. Not a word of condemnation nor remorse for this first falsehood passes between Jonathan and David on their next meeting, but the story speaks for itself. It was risky, to say the least—not to the fabricator but to his agent; and it stretched to the limits the bond of friendship that bound David to Jonathan.

After an emotional parting, David took to the hills, panic in his heart. It was just dawning on him that Saul's antagonism to him, no longer a matter of the occasional moody outburst, had become settled malice without release, and he was frightened. He had risen to fame with meteoric swiftness, and now just as quickly he was losing all he had acquired: his captaincy in the army, his wife, his place in the palace as the king's son-in-law and friend of the prince. This was an abrupt reversal of fortune, and as David had neither advisor nor experience to guide him, he fled into the hills pursued by fear.

After several nights in the open, little food, and a corroding anxiety, David came to Nob, the site of a colony of priests where he had often gone before to consult with the senior priest Ahimelech. He was hungry, and he decided to ask for food. Sensing that something was wrong, the old priest began to ask questions: 'Why did you come here all by yourself?' Again fear gripped David, and truth was the casualty: 'I am here on the king's business,' David answered. 'He told me not to let anyone know what he sent me to do. As for my men, I have told them to meet me at a certain place. Now, then, what supplies have you got? Give me five loaves of bread or anything else you have' (I Sam 21:1–3). Again David had lied. There was no secret mission. He had no men any more.

It got worse. The priests had no ordinary bread, only the consecrated bread of the Presence that had been removed from before the Lord and replaced with new bread. Ahimelech felt duty-bound to inquire whether David's men were ritually pure, and David swore blind that his fictitious men kept themselves from women even on ordinary missions, to say nothing of secret missions.

Fear drove him on from one falsehood to the next. After he had taken the bread, he realised that he had no weapon: 'Have you got a spear or a sword you can give me? The king's orders made me leave in such a hurry that I didn't have time to get my sword or any other weapon' (21:8). When Ahimelech reminded him that the sword of Goliath lay wrapped in a cloth behind the ephod, David immediately said, 'Give it to me. There is not a better sword anywhere!' (21:9). Before this incident Goliath's sword was last mentioned as being in David's tent after the defeat of the giant (I Sam 17:54). Presumably David himself had subsequently presented it to God in this sanctuary as a thank offering, a sign that 'the Lord does not need swords or spears to save his people' (17:47). Desperate now to save himself, David lied in order to take back the doubtful protection of Goliath's sword that he had previously dedicated to God.

Departing hastily from Nob, David fled recklessly to the enemy city of Gath, where he sought refuge with King Achish. His popularity, however, nearly ruined him. The court servants recognised him and reported to Achish, 'Isn't this David, the king of his country? This is the man about whom the women sang, as they danced, "Saul has killed his thousands, but David has killed tens of thousands"' (I Sam 21:11). Again David faced danger, and fear drove him to fabrication. Feigning insanity, he began to act like a madman, scribbling on the palace gates and dribbling saliva down his beard. The ruse worked, the king ordered him out of the city, and David escaped.

Fear, fabrication, fleeing for his life—it was becoming a pattern. What an ironic picture was emerging: not the shepherd boy, untried in battle, with confidence only in God, fearlessly facing Goliath with sling and stone; but the successful army officer, armed not with faith but with Goliath's sword, afraid for his life, fabricating lies and feigning madness to save his own skin. No longer trusting God to save him, David thought only of saving himself. He used every means—even lying—to do it.


## The Results of Lying


As so often happens when one fabricates stories, David was found out. Saul had seen through Jonathan's excuse; the servants of Achish had recognised David in Gath; and at Nob Saul's chief herdsman, Doeg the Edomite, happened to call to fulfil some religious obligation and saw him. At

the time he suspected nothing, but when he later learned of
the rift between Saul and David, his information was damn-
ing. He heard Saul dressing down his men for siding with
David and stepped forward with his story.

On his information the priest Ahimelech and the whole
colony of priests at Nob were summoned to the palace and
accused of plotting against Saul: 'Why are you and David
plotting against me? Why did you give him some food and
a sword, and consult God for him? Now he has turned
against me and is waiting for a chance to kill me!' (I Sam
21:13). For a second time, just as with Jonathan, David's
fabrications had endangered others while he himself escaped unscathed. With great dignity Ahimelech answered
Saul truthfully,

> Who of all your servants is as loyal as David, the
> king's son-in-law, captain of your bodyguard and
> highly respected in your household? Was that day the
> first time I inquired of God for him? Of course not!
> Let not the king accuse your servant or any of his
> father's family, for your servant knows nothing at all
> about this whole affair.
>
> (I Sam 22:13–15, NIV)

No hedging, no dodging, no prevarication, no extenuat-
ing circumstances. For his truthful answer Ahimelech
earned Saul's anger. Though Saul's own guards were unwilling to lift their hands against the priests of the Lord, Doeg
the Edomite obeyed Saul in his rage and singlehandedly
massacred Ahimelech and 85 priests along with their
families. Ahimelech died with truth on his lips.

### David's Remorse for Lying

Only one son of Ahimelech, Abiathar, escaped the sword
of Doeg that day to bring the news to David. It sobered him
on the spot, and with unhesitating candour and no qualifi-
cation he admitted his guilt: 'When I saw Doeg there that
day, I knew that he would be sure to tell Saul. So I am responsible for the death of all your relatives' (22:22). The
way that he said it showed that, even as he was deceiving
the old priest, there was a struggle going on in his conscience, aggravated by his being put in the power of an un-
scrupulous man like Doeg. In the end he named both evildoers with even-handed justice. He condemned Doeg and
he condemned himself. In Psalm 52 he wrote of Doeg and
his kind:

> Why do you boast, great man, of your evil?
>     God's faithfulness is eternal.
> You make plans to ruin others;
>     your tongue is like a sharp razor.
>     You are always inventing lies.
> You love evil more than good
>     and falsehood more than truth.
> You love to hurt people with your words, you liar!
>
> So God will ruin you for ever;
>     he will take hold of you and snatch you from your
>         home;
>     he will remove you from the world of the living.
>                                                  (Ps 52:1–5)

And in Psalm 34, still burning with remorse over his cow-
ardly humiliation when he feigned madness and fabricated
lies in the court of Achish, king of Gath, David took his

harp and sang. These lines from Psalm 34 look like a lesson
he may have learned from this incident:

> Come, my young friends, and listen to me,
>     and I will teach you to honour the Lord.
> Would you like to enjoy life?
>     Do you want long life and happiness?
> Then hold back from speaking evil
>     and from telling lies.
> Turn away from evil and do good;
>     strive for peace with all your heart.
>
> (Ps 34:11–14)

Like Ahimelech's courageous answer to Saul, this song
has lasted for three thousand years and still nerves people
to tell the truth even when they are starving with hunger,
even when they are paralysed with fear, even when danger
threatens their very lives. It is the only way for those who
follow him who said, 'I am the truth.'

**An enterprise is no greater than the values its people demonstrate.**

*I reckon my own life to be worth nothing to me. I only want to complete the mission and finish the work that the Lord Jesus gave me to do.*

— Paul in Acts 20:24

# VI
# Values
*I Samuel 22:1–4; II Samuel 23:13–17*

### The Cave of Adullam

David did not remain alone in the hills for long. His leadership ability, his military reputation, his attractive poetic temperament, in short his charisma—that indefinable quality of leadership that attracts followers and inspires them to dedicate themselves to a cause—inevitably drew others to him. When his brothers and his father's household discovered where he was hiding, they joined him, fleeing themselves from the unpredictable anger of Saul until David found them safe lodging in the neighbouring kingdom of Moab. Under Saul the country was being neglected or badly administered, and the number of discontented citizens grew. People who were oppressed or in debt or dissatisfied flocked to David, about 400 men in all, and he became their leader. Some, no doubt, suffered from genuine oppression, unjust debts, or justifiable dissatisfaction; others were probably parasites attracted by the free food and someone to take care of their needs. With this motley rabble David had to learn about leadership and mould a company of firm friends and well disciplined, able soldiers.

It was not an enviable way to start a political career. Not

only did David have to defend himself against Saul, not only did he have to fight the Philistines, but now he had to feed, clothe, train, and settle the disputes of 400 malcontents who looked to him for leadership. David described in song his problems as he hid from Saul in the cave of Adullam:

> I call to the LORD for help;
>   I plead with him.
> I bring him all my complaints;
>   I tell him all my troubles.
> When I am ready to give up,
>   he knows what I should do.
> In the path where I walk,
>   my enemies have hidden a trap for me.
> When I look beside me,
>   I see that there is no one to help me,
>   no one to protect me.
> No one cares for me.

(Ps 142:1–4)

## The Well of Bethlehem

One incident opens a window on those formative days. A company of Philistines, encamped in the Valley of Rephaim, had captured Bethlehem—David's home town —and stationed a garrison there. Doubly hemmed in by Saul and the Philistines, unable to move about his own country without restriction, David felt homesick and weary of the fugitive life. 'How I wish someone would bring me a drink of water from the well by the gate at Bethlehem!' he had sighed (II Sam 23:15). It was a natural wish, a longing for the values that he had learned to appreciate:

> LORD, I cry to you for help;

you, Lord, are my protector;
    you are all I want in this life.
Listen to my cry for help,
    for I am sunk in despair.
Save me from my enemies;
    they are too strong for me.
Set me free from my distress;
    then in the assembly of your people I will praise
        you.                                (Ps 142:5–7)

David was expressing a wish for peace from the
hardships, dangers, and tragedies of war and political
persecution, because he was a hunted man with a price on
his head:

I am surrounded by enemies,
    who are like man-eating lions.
Their teeth are like spears and arrows;
    their tongues are like sharp swords …
My enemies have spread a net to catch me;
    I am overcome with distress.
They dug a pit in my path,
    but fell into it themselves.

                                            (Ps 57:4, 6)

As he had painfully discovered with Jonathan and
Ahimelech, he had to think now not only about himself but
also about those who endangered themselves by joining
him and making him their leader. The strain was telling on
him, and he longed for peace: 'Be merciful to me, O God,
be merciful, because I come to you for safety. In the
shadow of your wings I find protection until the raging
storms are over' (Ps 57:1).

David was also voicing a wish for the regular supply of
creature comforts. The water in the well symbolised provision of the necessities of life—no need for foraging, no need

for scrounging, no need for risking lives just to gather food and drink. Water was always there for the taking, and everyone had enough.

His request for water was also a sigh for the simple things of home. At the well by the gate people gathered and exchanged local gossip and news. There the boys met the girls and laughed and teased, with older people indulgently looking on. The well symbolised acceptance and the warmth of belonging. It symbolised home. It held memories of parents, brothers and sisters, of the good times they had had together. It was a nostalgic wish that everything could be again as it had been—homely and happy—before his rapid rise to fame and sudden plunge from the king's favour.

When David thought of these things, of the well of Bethlehem in Philistine hands, and of himself unable to go, he made his wish.

## The High Cost of Freedom

Three of David's best and bravest men, three of the Thirty, men whose names we do not even know, overheard David's wish. Their attachment and devotion to him was so strong that they slipped away unnoticed to try to do something about his depression. Resolutely breaking through the enemy lines, they filled their water bottle at the well in Bethlehem, made the dangerous return journey without mishap, and presented David with his wish.

When David saw the water, he was dumbfounded. He had not meant his wish to be taken seriously. He had not even realised that he had been overheard. It must have done much to restore his flagging spirits to discover that he had men like those, men who without pay or direct request had risked their lives and behaved so generously. In that moment of self-awareness David discovered a further set of values that matter immensely to a leader. His men were devoted to him. He could not squander their devotion selfishly; instead he must channel their devotion into the cause of freeing Israel from its enemies. When he saw the water, David knew that he could not drink it. In that moment of self-awareness he knew too that he could never go back to Bethlehem; he could never recapture those simple days of herding sheep in the hills and relaxing in the evening at the well by the gate; he could never recapture the pleasurable life in Saul's palace nor his position as trusted captain of Saul's bodyguards. When he saw the water, he saw not clear, cool, fresh water satisfying a private nostalgic longing for home and peace, freedom and plenty; instead he saw water crimson red, a symbol of the life blood risked to bring it to him, a symbol of the ideal of freedom for which they all suffered and fought. He was overcome by deep emotion and refused to drink: 'Lord, I could never drink this! It would be like drinking the blood of these men who risked their lives!' (II Sam 23:17).

He did not drink the water—rather, in an inspired act he poured it out before the Lord as an oblation, a drink offering. He transformed what had begun as a nostalgic wish into an act of worship, into a prayer for God's protection, an act of thanksgiving for his past provision. He took up his harp and sang:

> I have complete confidence, O God;
> > I will sing and praise you!
> Wake up, my soul!
> > Wake up, my harp and lyre!
> > I will wake up the sun.
> I will thank you, O Lord, among the nations.
> > I will praise you among the peoples.

Your constant love reaches the heavens;
    your faithfulness touches the skies.
Show your greatness in the sky, O God,
    and your glory over all the earth.

                                    (Ps 57:7–11)

David was learning the values that would be important to his cause; he could not consume the water selfishly, because of its cost. Perhaps the three mighty men who had brought the water thought, 'What a waste!' when they saw it soak into the ground. A moment's reflection, however, would have assured them that a man who set such a value on their actions and their gift as to elevate them to an act of worship would never waste anything. The seeming waste guaranteed the success of their cause, guaranteed the value and preservation of all that the water symbolised—plenty, peace, and freedom.

David took all that he had and especially the thing that he valued the most and gave it back to God as His. The Apostle Paul takes up this thought and personalises it. Twice he speaks of his own life as a drink offering which he was ready to pour out in sacrificial service for God and for others (Phil 2:17; II Tim 4:6). In his case the stimulus, far greater than the daring deed of the Three, was the price paid by Jesus, crucified to set him free, free from bigotry, free from violence, free from racial pride. He called these the law of sin and death, and his freedom was eternal life. The old values he counted as refuse in the light of the liberated life he found through Jesus. The only worthy response was to pour out his life—like David pouring out the water from the well of Bethlehem—as an offering in the service of his Lord and his people.

**The leader himself needs to be led by God.**

*From such terrible dangers of death he saved us, and will save us; and we have placed our hope in him that he will save us again.*

— Paul in II Cor 1:10

# VII
# Prayer and Decisions
## *I Samuel chapter 23*


No interpretation of David's career can ignore the fact that a great part of his success comes from his awareness of—and familiarity with—the spiritual dimension in all of life, private and public. There is no question about his military genius, his way with people, and a whole battery of other remarkable gifts. But David would neither have been the man he was nor have built what he achieved if it had not been for this extra dimension in life. The Psalms provide the greatest evidence of how much he prayed, but the narrative also shows a man who believed that God was real and that God was involved in the affairs of men.


### The Rescue of Keilah

The town of Keilah was a case in point. It was an Israelite town that was just gathering in its harvest. The enemy Philistines sent out raiding parties to loot the threshing floors and carry off the grain. Saul should have sent his army to offer protection, but he didn't. Although he had no responsibility in the matter and although Saul was likely to misinterpret his intervention, David, the patriot, wanted to do something. He prayed for guidance and felt that he should act (verses 1–2), but when he put it to his men, they opposed him: 'We have enough to be afraid of here in Judah; it will be much worse if we go to Keilah and attack the Philistine forces!' (verse 3). In spite of their discouraging advice, he prayed again and decided to proceed with his plan. David's men attacked and defeated the Philistines, captured their livestock, and relieved the town.

His very success, however, created two difficulties. It put the citizens in the compromising position of appearing to be linked with David. This would do them no good with Saul. It also put David in a walled town where he would be very vulnerable if caught between the thumb of an outside attack and forefinger of a frightened citizenry. In fact, when Saul heard that David had gone to Keilah, he said, 'God has put him in my power. David has trapped himself by going into a walled town with fortified gates' (verse 7). He immediately mobilised his troops to besiege Keilah and capture David and his men.

David was frustrated. With divine encouragement he had successfully attacked the Philistines and rescued Keilah, only to create more trouble for them and himself. With the memory of the massacre of the priests of Nob still fresh in his mind, he prayed again. Abiathar, the sole survivor of Saul's revenge at Nob, had joined David and brought with him into the camp the ephod, the embroidered vestment worn by the priests when asking direction from God. Through Abiathar David now consulted God again and learned that Saul would attack and that the people of Keilah would surrender him to Saul. Once again David and his men, now numbering about 600, took to the hills. Eager to act for the welfare of people, but in difficulty with a system that crowded him out, David resorted to the God who controls men and events, and God helped him to escape.

### Treachery in the Desert of Ziph

From the walled town of Keilah to the desert strongholds and the hills of the Desert of Ziph David eluded the army of Saul. While he was hiding at Horesh in the desert, encouragement came from an unexpected source. Jonathan had slipped away from Saul's army and come to assure David of God's protection. 'Don't be afraid,' he said. 'My father Saul won't be able to harm you. He knows very well that you are the one who will be the king of Israel and that I will be next in rank to you' (verse 17). From the same palace the father had set out to capture and kill him and the son had come to reassure him. Jonathan and David shared the conviction that men in leadership could get guidance and insight from God, and Jonathan had once again risked his life to pass through the lines of armed sentries and help David find strength in God.

Not everyone in the Desert of Ziph had the same attitude as Jonathan. Ziphite informers, trying to court the king's favour, betrayed David's whereabouts to Saul: 'David is hiding in our territory at Horesh on Mount Hachilah, in the southern part of the Judaean wilderness. We know, Your Majesty, how much you want to capture him; so come to our territory, and we will make sure that you catch him' (verses 19–20). The situation David had feared inside Keilah began to be re-enacted even in the open countryside. What could he do? Humanly speaking there was nothing to do but run, but for David there was still one way he could take. He could go to God, and he did. Psalm 54 records a prayer that might have been offered on this occasion:

Save me by your power, O God;
   set me free by your might!

Hear my prayer, O God;
    listen to my words!
Proud men are coming to attack me;
    cruel men are trying to kill me—
    men who do not care about God.
But God is my helper.
    The Lord is my defender.
May God use their own evil to punish my enemies.
    He will destroy them because he is faithful.

I will gladly offer you a sacrifice, O Lord;
    I will give you thanks
    because you are good.
You have rescued me from all my troubles,
    and I have seen my enemies defeated.

### Pursuit in the Desert of Maon

David fled south into the Desert of Maon with Saul in pursuit. Saul and his men were on one side of a mountain, while on the other side of the mountain David and his men were hurrying to get away. Saul's army was closing in on them and about to capture them when a message arrived from the palace at Gibeah: 'Come back at once! The Philistines are invading the country!' (verse 27). Then Saul broke off his pursuit of David and went to fight the Philistines.

From this dramatic escape David learned that God has more ways than one of answering prayer. Just as God defied human wisdom and enabled David without benefit of sword or shield to kill Goliath with a slingshot, so once again he protected David without the human defences of walled city or stone fortress. In learning to consult God, David had become the realist who saw life as a whole and

took into account all the factors. He had learned to acknow-
ledge the spiritual dimension in all of life and to operate in
conscious co-operation with, and dependence on, God.
Though his circumstances got no better, his leadership became surer and the earlier signs of panic disappeared.

**Excuses should never be elevated in our mind to the status of reasons.**

*Be concerned above everything else with the Kingdom of God and with what he requires of you, and he will provide you with all these other things.*

— Jesus in Matthew 6:33

# VIII
# Principle
*I Samuel chapters 24, 26*

Field Marshal John Okello, who carried out the revolution in Zanzibar in 1964, was asked how he, an ordinary soldier, had learned to stage a successful revolution. He replied, 'It's all in the Bible.' He was not being facetious. In a period of about 300 years, Judah and Israel between them had a dozen violent revolutions, or on average one every 25 years. The neighbouring states were just as unstable politically. By contrast, at the beginning of the Kingdom of Israel almost a century passed without internal revolution, a peaceful century all the more remarkable since the Kingdom was just emerging from being the loose collection of tribes described in the book of Judges.

Without doubt David's loyalty to one principle in the face of many pressures to abandon it produced this unity and stability. On principle David refused to harm the one whom God had chosen to be king: 'The Lord forbid that I should try to harm the one whom the Lord has made king!' (I Sam 26:11), he repeated again and again, even when his men were continually being harassed, even when he could easily have used the argument of self-defence to justify retaliating against Saul's murderous attacks on him. Because of a religious conviction David would not stoop to violent revolution as the means by which he might become king.

## Principle and Opportunity

In the Desert of En Gedi David used a network of caves in
the hillside to hide his men and store his supplies. While
Saul with 3,000 men chosen from all Israel was pursuing
David, he happened to stop to rest in the mouth of a cave
where David and some of his men were hiding. From the
dark recesses at the back of the cave they could see Saul,
but he could not see them. David's men urged him, 'This is
your chance! The Lord has told you that he would put your
enemy in your power and you could do to him whatever you
wanted to' (I Sam 24:4). David took out a knife and went
forward with great stealth not to kill the king but only to cut
off a piece of Saul's robe and creep back. His men were
dumbfounded. They had been waiting for an opportunity
to kill Saul, to end their troubles, and to put David in
power. But David refused: 'May the Lord keep me from
doing any harm to my master, whom the Lord chose as
king!' (24:6).

For David, opportunity did not cancel principle. His men
argued that this was his chance. They argued that the very
opportunity was evidence of God's direction and therefore
a reason for setting aside principle. David, however,
thought differently. He believed that if principle and opportunity clashed, the opportunity must pass and the principle must remain.

## Principle and Popular Support

Neither did the strong backing of popular support cancel
principle. David had 600 good and loyal men supporting

him, and with so many urging him on, capturing Saul must have seemed right. David, however, did not subscribe to the common concept of leadership—'find out what the people want and lead them to it'. He did not say, as many do in effect, 'I am your leader; I will follow you.' He did not abdicate from his principle just because he had popular support.

Instead of violence he tried talking. He allowed Saul out of the cave and confronted him verbally:

> Why do you listen to people who say that I am trying to harm you? You can see for yourself that just now in the cave the Lord put you in my power. Some of my men told me to kill you, but I felt sorry for you and said that I would not harm you in the least, because you are the one whom the Lord chose to be king. Look, my father, look at the piece of your robe I am holding! I could have killed you, but instead I only cut this off. This should convince you that I have no thought of rebelling against you or of harming you.
>
> (I Sam 24:9–11)

David's non-violent tactics worked. When Saul recognised David and realised that he had spared him, he wept with shame and called off his man-hunt.

> You are right, and I am wrong. You have been so good to me, while I have done such wrong to you! Today you have shown how good you are to me, because you did not kill me, even though the Lord put me in your power. How often does a man catch his enemy and then let him get away unharmed? The Lord bless you for what you have done to me today! Now I am sure that you will be king of Israel and that the kingdom will continue under your rule.
>
> (24:17–20)

David had achieved his goal without using violence. For the time being Saul called off the man-hunt.

## Principle and Treachery

Saul's penitence, however, was short-lived. Ignoring his promise, he soon returned with his army to the Desert of Ziph to hunt down David again. This time Saul's army was camped in a valley. David looked down on it from a hill top at night and saw Saul's tent in the centre of the camp surrounded by his men. He had a sudden inspiration. Taking one man, Abishai, with him, he crept past the sleeping guards, right through the enemy lines, until he found Saul sleeping near Abner, the commander of the army. His man Abishai urged him, 'God has put your enemy in your power tonight' (I Sam 26:8). But David refused to harm Saul. Not even Saul's treachery made him feel justified in leaving his principle. Saul had broken his promise to leave him alone, and many another man would have regarded himself as free from any obligation to keep faith. David's principle, however, was held before God, and man's unreliability only reinforced his need to be true. He told Abishai, 'By the living Lord, I know that the Lord himself will kill Saul, either when his time comes to die a natural death or when he dies in battle. The Lord forbid that I should try to harm the one whom the Lord has made king!' (I Sam 26:10–11). Instead of striking Saul, he contented himself with taking Saul's spear and water jar as a way of getting talks started again.

## Principle and Proxy

Nor did David allow himself to violate his principle by proxy. As they stood over the sleeping Saul and Abner, Abishai had said, 'Now let me plunge his own spear through him and pin him to the ground with just one blow— I won't have to strike twice!' (26:8). Abishai's offer to spear Saul put David into another temptation. If David was unwilling to kill Saul himself, Abishai was willing to do the dirty work and to take the blame. He understood the political risks for David. He was willing to risk banishment or imprisonment for his master, confident that when David came to power, he would make things right. David need never soil his hands in this affair. David, however, refused his offer; he did not imagine that by turning away his head while the deed was done that he would not be implicated. Unlike Pilate at the crucifixion of Jesus, David would not take a basin, wash his hands, and say, 'All right, you do it. I am innocent.'

## Principle and Need

In David's book even need did not displace principle. He could have justly argued, 'My men need respite from this underground existence.' More widely he could have argued, 'This country needs a new government.' It was all too true: Saul harassed his men unjustly; he administered the country poorly; and the Philistines constantly violated Israel's frontiers. The country needed change, but even such need took second place to David's principle. He was not content with fair-weather ethics, conveniently forgotten or rationalised when the going was rough. His grip on God's law was stronger than that.

## The Validity of his Principle

David's principle of loyalty to God's appointed leader implied a philosophy of history that saw God as the ultimate controller of events. The prophet Daniel stated it to Nebuchadnezzar: 'God is wise and powerful! Praise him for ever and ever. He controls the times and the seasons; he makes and unmakes kings; it is he who gives wisdom and understanding' (Dan 2:20–21). The Apostle Paul restated this concept in the New Testament: 'Everyone must obey the state authorities, because no authority exists without God's permission, and the existing authorities have been put there by God' (Rom 13:1). Jesus hinted at the same outlook when Pilate said to him. 'Remember, I have the authority to set you free and also to have you crucified.' Jesus answered, 'You have authority over me only because it was given to you by God' (John 19:10–11). David based his principle on a conviction that runs throughout the Bible: God ultimately controls history. Governments are primarily God's concern, and David had no wish to abrogate to himself what he felt belonged to God.

David not only refused to forget his principle and kill Saul, he also worked in every way possible to show his positive attitude to Saul's whole family. He talked whenever he could to bring about reconciliation. Standing at the edge of the camp with Saul's spear and water bottle, he once again confronted Saul with his innocence and forced him to confess his guilt (I Sam 26:13–25). David cherished his friendship with Saul's son Jonathan. He regarded as inviolate his marriage to Saul's daughter Michal even after Saul had given her to another husband (II Sam 3:13–16). When Saul and Jonathan were killed on the field, he executed the man who reported the matter and claimed responsibility. Instead of rejoicing as he might, he composed a lament and specifically ordered it to be taught to his own tribe of Judah:

> Saul and Jonathan—in life they were loved and gracious, and in death they were not parted. They were swifter than eagles, they were stronger than lions. O daughters of Israel, weep for Saul, who clothed you in scarlet and finery, who adorned your garments with ornaments of gold. How the mighty have fallen in battle!
>
> (II Sam 1:23–25, NIV)

When Saul's son Ishbosheth was made king of the northern part of the country by his general Abner, David took no action against him except to defend himself when attacked. When eventually both the general and Ishbosheth were assassinated, he disassociated himself from both acts in the strongest possible language (II Sam chapters 3–4). When he himself ruled over the whole country, he sought out Saul's lame grandson Mephibosheth and brought him to the palace and maintained him all his life. David consistently acted towards Saul's family on the principle of generosity and loyalty.

Sticking to his convictions did not come easily, but David's adherence to principle became a binding force in the nation. David saw clearly the need to build unity. He wanted to win and not antagonise the tribe of Benjamin, who had given Israel their first king. What would any tribe think if one of their people was the ruler and a man from another tribe assassinated him and took over the government? Africa in the 1960s provides the answer. The civil war in Nigeria had just such moves underlying it, and the

hatred and antagonism engendered will take a generation
to work out. Sudan, Togo, Dahomey, Gabon, Zanzibar,
Ghana, the Congo and Sierra Leone—all have seen the
army usurp the civilian government and take over the running of their countries. In other countries abortive military
mutinies have been quelled. But David rejected this violent
path to power, and it is significant that half a century later,
when the country was again divided, Benjamin was the one
tribe that stayed with Judah while the other ten seceded (I
Kings 12:21–24). Even after he was dead, his waiting
patiently for God's help and his adherence to the principle
of loyalty to the God-appointed ruler were remarkably
rewarded.

David had not heard Jesus say, 'All who take the sword
will die by the sword' (Matt 26:52). David did not know that
Jesus would refuse to sanction violence even when he was
unjustly arrested. He had no inkling of the Resurrection
that made the victim victor. Yet he as the victim also became the victor, with a similar confidence in God that kept
him true to his principle to the end, and built an element of
stability into the nation's life.

**When you lose your temper, you always lose more than your temper.**

*If you become angry, do not let your anger lead you into sin.... Don't give the devil a chance.*

*— Paul in Ephesians 4:26*

# IX
# Temper
*I Samuel chapter 25*

David met many different people during his life. Two of the most colourful were a greatly contrasting husband and wife, Nabal and Abigail. The husband's anger almost provoked David to a terrible massacre—which was prevented only by Nabal's wife's pragmatism and charm.

### The Rich Fool of the Old Testament

Nabal was a prototype of the man who says to himself, 'Lucky man! You have all the good things you need for many years. Take life easy, eat, drink, and enjoy yourself!'—but who is never satisfied (Luke 12:19). He had 4,000 cattle, 3,000 sheep, 1,000 goats—all with access to the extensive pastureland needed to graze them. He was descended from the old aristocratic family of Caleb; by any standards he was extremely rich.

His lands, however, were set in an area in which stock theft was a major hazard both from local people and raiding parties from neighbouring states. His own government was weak, and security in the area was ineffective. In these circumstances, David and his outlawed band of 600 men provided protection. In true Robin Hood style, they

magnanimously took it upon themselves to protect the Israelite farms and their stock.

Nabal benefitted from this unexpected security force,
and a good relationship developed between his herdsmen
and David's company. Feeding 600 men on the run was no
easy task and, not unnaturally, David received gifts in kind
from the farms that owed their security and prosperity to
him.

In the year in question, when it was sheep-shearing time
for Nabal's 3,000 sheep, and in anticipation of the custom-
ary feast, David sent out 10 of his young men to the farm
with this message:

> David sends you greetings, my friend, with his best
> wishes for you, your family and all that is yours. He
> heard that you were shearing your sheep, and he
> wants you to know that your shepherds have been
> with us and we did not harm them. Nothing that be-
> longed to them was stolen ... Just ask them, and they
> will tell you. We have come on a feast day, and David
> asks you to receive us kindly. Please give what you
> can to us your servants and to your dear friend David.
> (verses 6–8)

It was not much to ask, especially in a society where tradi-
tionally the poor were provided for at harvest time.

When Nabal heard their little speech, he came out in his
true colours. He totally lost his temper and insulted them.
Josephus, the Jewish historian, says he snarled and snap-
ped. Not only did he decline or offer excuses—but he
blasted David, his father, and his family, and insinuated the
worst he could about David's relations with Saul by calling
him a runaway slave: 'I'm not going to take my bread and
water and the animals I have slaughtered for my shearers,
and give them to men who come from I don't know where!'

It was not pleasant. It showed what an ill-natured, ill-tempered, ill-mannered, boorish and badly behaved man he was. He stepped straight into the character of the big-mouthed, swaggering miser, eloquent in expletives, of which almost any literature has its example. Success and prosperity had been his great test. It could have made him a better man, but it made him worse. He was successful in farming. He had a good-looking wife, but he still did not have enough. He should have been expanding with the easier circumstances, becoming more relaxed, more friendly, more generous and more approachable. Instead he became harder, more cocksure and arrogant, more self-centred and grasping, more stubborn and loud-mouthed and more of a fool—which is in fact the meaning of the name Nabal.

His feast was princely, but only for his own benefit. It would seem that his wife did not matter very much to him. Once he had her, he took her for granted; she could be away from the house and the feast, and he did not even notice. His servants said he was so pig-headed that he would not listen to anybody. At the end of the story when his wife told him how she had saved them all from disaster, he did not thank her but had a fit, went into a coma and died 10 days later from the shock.

What caused the shock? It could have been the loss of all the provisions. It could have been the discovery that he was so near to death. Or it could have been that he just could not bear being indebted to his wife for anything.

Nabal's character is clear. From our knowledge of his many counterparts, we can imagine him regularly fulminating over Abigail's extravagance and waste in her house-keeping, and at the same time wanting fine fare served daily. No doubt he was adept at casting aspersions on Abigail's family and regarding them in his self-righteousness as immoral scum. When she kept quiet (perhaps the only way she knew how to cope) he would rage because he was not answered.

His servants would suffer from his unjust accusations about their characters, their origins, and their work. The only thing worse than his tirades would be his sullen silences when everyone feared what would burst from the cloud that was forming about his brow. Nabal was his name, and folly was with him.

### A Patient Man Loses Control

When David's men returned with Nabal's answer, he was furious. Although he had been able to keep his head under the great stress of being unjustly pursued by Saul, Nabal took him off his guard. Although he had been careful to restrain his men from taking any action that would injure the king, he was stung into mobilising them for the merciless massacre of all on Nabal's farm the very same day.

He set out to answer a fool according to his folly. He committed himself to revenge, even if it meant the murder of innocent people. He did not think of the seeds of bitterness he would sow for years to come on the impulse of an angry moment. He imagined that a second temper lost could cure the first. We can see it all in the turmoil of his inner thoughts: 'Why did I ever protect that fellow's property out here in the wilderness? Not a thing that belonged to him was stolen, and this is how he pays me back for the help I gave him! May God strike me dead if I don't kill every last one of those men before morning!' (verses 21–22). Mercifully, there was someone thinking straight that day.

## A Wife Fit for a King

All was not folly in Nabal's household. Abigail his wife, who must have been the joy of her father, saved the day.

Nabal and Abigail are about the strangest combination of husband and wife one could ever imagine. How they could ever have come to be married defies speculation. On the surface it seems as though that was the one occasion on which her intelligence failed her. Why did she marry him? Was it his money? Was it an arranged marriage? Was he a good actor, playing the noble suitor until he got what he wanted? Perhaps he was different as a young man. Whatever the reason, she had made her bed and had to lie in it. The amazing thing is that she did not become sour with him.

This incident shows what stuff she was made of. She was a person of decisive action. She knew her stock and her kitchen and had supplies laid in to cope with emergencies. She had her servants' complete confidence; they would do anything for her. It was one of them who reported to her what had transpired between David and Nabal.

She did not lose a minute. She organised her party and her goods with arithmetical precision for David's men: 5 sheep, 5 sacks of grain, 100 bushels of raisins, 200 loaves of bread, 200 cakes of dried figs and 2 large leather bags of wine. She was so well organised, the heart of her husband might well have trusted in her! She loaded it all on donkeys, sent it ahead with her servants to pacify David's anger and came later with all her wisdom and charm.

It was a classic meeting. She made the longest recorded speech of any woman in the Bible. Her 300 words are a veritable gem of a public relations exercise. Practitioners today give rules for influencing people without giving offence, but without having read those books, she used all the rules!

1. Talk about your own mistakes before criticising the other person:

> 'Please, sir, listen to me! Let me take the blame. Please, don't pay any attention to Nabal, that good-for-nothing! He is exactly what his name means—a fool! I wasn't there when your servants arrived, sir' (verses 24–25).

2. Call attention to the other's mistakes indirectly:

> 'It is the Lord who has kept you from taking revenge and killing your enemies. And now I swear to you by the living Lord that your enemies and all who want to harm you will be punished like Nabal' (verse 26).

3. Make the fault seem easy to correct:

> 'Please, sir, accept this present I have brought you, and give it to your men' (verse 27).

4. Use honest appreciation:

> 'Please, forgive me, sir, for any wrong I have done. The Lord will make you king, and your descendants also, because you are fighting his battles' (verse 28).

5. Give the dog a good name—a reputation to live up to:

> 'You will not do anything evil as long as you live. If anyone should attack you and try to kill you, the Lord your God will keep you safe, as a man guards a precious treasure. As for your enemies, however, he will throw them away, as a man hurls stones with his catapult' (verses 28–29).

6. Let the other man save his face:

> 'And when the Lord has done all the good things he
> has promised you and has made you king of Israel,
> then you will not have to feel regret or remorse, sir,
> for having killed without cause or for having taken
> your own revenge. And when the Lord has blessed
> you, sir, please do not forget me' (verses 30–31).

7. Make the other person happy at the thing you suggest:

> 'David said to her, "Praise the Lord, the God of Isra-
> el, who sent you today to meet me! Thank God for
> your good sense and for what you have done today in
> keeping me from the crime of murder and from taking
> my own revenge"' (verse 32–33).

With all her womanly skill, though she did not hesitate to
admit her husband's faults, she defended him both by what
she did and how she did it. Although she felt it wise not to
advise him of her intentions beforehand (verse 19), she did
tell him at the earliest suitable moment afterwards and hid
nothing (verses 36–37). It was too much for mean, miserly
Nabal. Instead of thanking her for her timely intervention,
he had a stroke and died. Scripture does not specifically re-
veal what gave him his stroke, but it shows how foolishly his
heart was imprisoned by his miserliness.

Neither her resourcefulness nor her intelligence and
beauty were lost on David. A person who could so quickly
penetrate through his foolish temper and point out where
his real interests lay was a person worth having around.
When he heard that Nabal had died, he proposed marriage,
and she accepted. How much she influenced the man he became is not known. David's was not a happy household,
and undoubtedly she had plenty of opportunity to show her

resourcefulness and many more tempers to cool. We do know, however, that neither she nor her children figure in the later, more sordid doings of David's unhappy court.

**People who are true to themselves cannot be false to others.**

*Jesus said, 'If anyone wants to come with me, he must forget self, take up his cross every day, and follow me. For whoever wants to save his own life will lose it, but whoever loses his life for my sake will save it.*

— Luke 9:23–24

# X
# Self-interest
*I Samuel chapters 27–29*

### A Counsel of Despair

There are some really low points in the career of David. One of them came towards the end of his outlaw period. The long pursuit was wearing him down; looking after a growing band of men who were already discontented or in some kind of distress was taking its toll. All his efforts to be conciliatory towards Saul proved abortive. It was getting beyond endurance. He had no desire to lead an opposition group, or a resistance movement, or a subversive gang. But the way the government handled things seemed to leave him with few alternatives. He said to himself, 'One of these days Saul will kill me. The best thing for me to do is to escape to Philistia. Then Saul will give up looking for me in Israel, and I will be safe' (I Sam 27:1).

Now the Philistines were public enemy number one as far as Israel was concerned. So David was making a decision to go over to the other side when he virtually hired himself and his private army of 600 men to Achish, king of the city state of Gath in the Gaza strip. He did it out of sheer self-interest. No doubt he felt driven to it by the frustrations he was experiencing. There was no opportunity to use his considerable ability in the service of his own country. Bitterness was creeping up on him. We have the impression that God was receding into the background, because there is no mention of him or any record of David consulting the Lord either through a priest or in any other way. He felt alone and so reverted to his own strategies. His truthfulness and high principles suffered in the process.

## A Course of Duplicity

Once David had made self-interest the principle he was following, a number of other things also began to deteriorate. Truth became the first casualty. To begin with David's private army was stationed in the royal city of Gath under the watchful eye of the king, but David's men, accustomed to the free life of adventurers, soon chafed under this restriction. To deal with this situation, David made a convincing argument about his people causing too much inconvenience to the king in Gath and suggested that they be moved to another, smaller town. Achish was taken in and said that they could be stationed at Ziklag, some miles further south.

Once they had escaped the supervision of Achish, David quickly set to work. He sent men out on raids on tribes further south who were traditional enemies of Israel. In these raids his men acquired considerable booty of sheep, oxen, asses, camels and clothing. Whenever Achish called and saw the increasing livestock, he asked where David had raided this time. Invariably David kept a straight face and said that he had raided one of the settlements in the Negev of Judah or one of her allies. David and his men prospered, but truth became a casualty.

Respect for life also suffered. In order to conceal his lies to Achish, people were indiscriminately massacred. David strictly instructed his men to put everyone—men, women, and children—to the sword. No one was to be left alive to tell the tale.

During this period David clearly lowered the value that he set on personal relationships. He professed allegiance to Achish, and Achish trusted him. Totally deceived about the source of David's increasing wealth, the Philistine king made him his permanent bodyguard. When his fellow Philistine commanders challenged his trust of David, Achish defended him: 'He has been with me for quite a long time now. He has done nothing I can find fault with since the day he came over to me' (I Sam 29:3). To David himself Achish said, 'I consider you as loyal as an angel of God' (29:9).

Nothing else in David's career matched the murderous, cheating, hoodwinking skulduggery of the 16 months that he spent at Ziklag. No doubt David rationalised his behaviour. He was fighting Israel's enemies. He was protecting his men from Saul, increasing their wealth, consolidating his position after years on the run. He had never had it so good before. After he had once begun to be controlled by self-interest, any number of good reasons must have seemed to support his actions.

All through this period, the only mention of God comes from the lips of the heathen king Achish when he naïvely protests David's honesty (29:6, 9). At this time David wrote no psalms. He seems to have hung up his harp and lost his song. When David forgot God, the spirit of seeking personal advantage began to undermine the things that made him great.


## A Climax of Disillusionment

Although the provocation was strong to adopt the creed of

self-interest, the consequences were nearly disastrous. The
time came when the Philistines prepared to march on Israel, and Achish said to David, 'Of course you understand
that you and your men are to fight on my side' (I Sam 28:1).
David had deserted to keep from fighting Saul; now he was
being forced by the very spirit that he had lived by for 16
months to go into the Philistine front line against Saul and
all Israel. He found himself on the wrong side.

Mercifully, the other Philistine commanders did not
want to risk having traitors in their ranks and asked, 'What
are these Hebrews doing here?' and insisted that they be
sent back (I Sam 29:3). David's former prowess under Saul
was well known, and his new allegiance was suspect.

He was now disowned by both sides, in a spiritual desert
with nowhere to go but back. He had played out his own de-
ceptions, and they recoiled on his own head and shamed his
benefactor. He was at an all-time low and might well have
disappeared as another one who showed great promise but
went the way of all flesh, drowning his potential glory in the
flood of self-interest.

At this point there was little to choose between David
and Saul. Neither seemed to provide hope for Israel. Both
were on the track of self-interest. It was a dangerous and a
downward track—but the end was not yet.

**To face failure and recover is the best preparation for a leader who wants to understand people.**

*All I want is to know Christ and to experience the power of his resurrection, to share in his sufferings and become like him in his death, in the hope that I myself will be raised from death to life.*

— Paul in Philippians 3:10–11.

# XI
# Recovering from Failure
*I Samuel 30*

### When All Seemed Lost

David had one step lower to go. He had been outlawed and hounded out of Israel by Saul. He was rejected by the Philistines and excluded from the ranks of their fighting men. All he had left were his own men and they turned on him also. This is how it happened.

Sent away by the Philistines, he made his way back to Ziklag, their base in recent times. The town was a smoking ruin. The wives and children of all his men had been taken captive, his two wives among them. All their livestock and goods had been plundered; there was nothing and nobody left. All seemed lost: 'David and his men started crying and did not stop until they were completely exhausted ... David was now in great trouble, all because his men were very bitter about losing their children, and they were threatening to stone him' (verses 4, 6).

A more lonely person is hard to imagine. If he had sowed the wind, he was now reaping the whirlwind. The raider had been raided; all he had accumulated was gone. Not a shred remained and his men turned on him threatening slow, cruel death by starvation. For the first time he was completely helpless. He had failed in everything he set out to do, and he had a mocking conscience that told him that he was only being given his own medicine. He had asked for it all; he alone was responsible.

Failure is a great test of a man. What did David do?

## The Way Back

David strengthened himself in the Lord, his God (verse 6). He turned right around to what he had long known but recently ignored. He opened heart, mind, soul and strength to God. There was no one else to whom he could go but to the Lord, and he was humble enough to go. We do not have the exact prayer he used, but its elements must be scattered throughout the Psalms.

Whatever the words David used, the effect was immediate. He called the priest who had served him in earlier days and urged him to ask the Lord whether or not he should go after the raiders.

This was a great change! He was ready to pursue and recover what had been taken or, if the Lord wished, to stay and accept his loss—and along with it, perhaps even the threat of death by stoning. If the mark of true repentance is the willingness to face and accept the consequences of our actions, David was repentant that day at Ziklag, for he was ready to bear with meekness the hand of God. He did not struggle to assert himself and move heaven and earth to get back where he had been.

As he and his men waited for Abiathar the priest to indicate the mind of the Lord, it must have been a tense moment on which hung the issue of life or death, the fulfilment or the denial of the promise of God in David's call to be king. The word came back, 'Go after them; you will catch them and rescue the captives' (verse 8).

With everything and everyone he had, David set off in pursuit. The men, already wearied by the long journey from the Philistine battle lines, were driven to superhuman efforts. As far as David was concerned, he was out to undo —as far as he could—the damage his own conduct had caused. For one-third of the men the demands were too much, but the rest pressed on and David recovered all. Nothing was missing.

This was mercy from God, not prowess. David knew this and was learning the lesson. David quickly squashed the mercenary self-interest which dared to raise its head among the men, who constantly wanted to penalise those who had remained behind:

> 'My brothers, you can't do this with what the Lord has given us. He kept us safe and gave us victory over the raiders. No one can agree with what you say! All must share alike: whoever stays behind with the supplies gets the same share as the one who goes into battle.' David made this a rule and it has been followed in Israel ever since.
>
> (verses 23–25)

The old consideration for others was returning and generosity was not far behind. He sent part of the spoil recovered to more than a dozen places where he and his men had roamed. The accumulator was becoming the dispenser again.

## Two Defeats

It is significant that two defeats took place at the same time. One was David's defeat at Ziklag. The other was the defeat of Saul and the armies of Israel on Mount Gilboa. Saul's defeat was the end of a long tragic trail of failures that could be traced back to uncorrected self-interest in the earlier years of the king's life. Saul did not know how to recover from failure and thereafter he only had the appearance of life and power. He died in fact years before he was buried.

For David, on the other hand, his defeat was also a death out of which came the resurrection we have traced. The defeat happened just before he became king, and the influence of this experience on his coming to the throne was very great. He might have been crowned a proud man and the story might have ended like Saul's. Instead he was crowned a humble man and lived to become a legend to his people for centuries. Ziklag and what happened there was a major key to his greatness.

Historically, this was the beginning of a concept that proved to be very important for Jews, for Christians, and for the world. It took centuries for it to crystalise, but in time David became the ideal king to whom future generations in Israel looked back with longing for the things he represented. Around the time of Isaiah, when the deportation of Northern Israel took place and Judah fell on evil times, the idea began to grow of a king like David who would come in the future to restore the kingdom to what God intended.

When Jesus Christ came, his talk was all about the kingdom of God—and he was called the Son of David. His own approach was on the same terms as David's. Jesus offered himself without coercion to the people and declared that those who received him entered the kingdom of God. He allowed himself to be crucified because the majority said, 'We will not have this man to reign over us!' His Resurrection and Ascension are compared with the coronation of David (Eph 4:8). The spread of the gospel of the Kingdom is linked directly to the promises made to David (Acts 15:16–18).

It is a revolutionary concept, the kingdom of God in which there are only voluntary citizens. And the seed of that world-changing idea began with David.

**Authority has ultimately to be won from those over whom it is exercised.**

*Jesus said, 'If one of you wants to be great, he must be the servant of the rest; and if one of you wants to be first, he must be the slave of all.'*

— Mark 10:43–44

# XII
# Rule by Consent
*II Samuel 2, 3, 5; I Chronicles 11–12*

What happens when a man gets power? It poses a great test, especially if his rise to power is sharp and sudden. If a man's salary increases ten times in one year, he faces a great test of character. If a man has been hunted, persecuted and pursued for many years and then suddenly becomes undisputed leader, that will show what is in a man. This is what happened to David. After years of being outlawed he became king at the age of 30 over his own tribe of Judah. Seven years later he became king over all Israel. His career to that point showed that his coming to power could go either very badly or very well.

### Reaction to his Predecessor's Death

While David and his men recovered their wives and children from the Amalekites, the Philistines had marched onward toward Israel. They defeated the Israelite army at Mount Gilboa and killed Saul and three of his sons, including Jonathan. When the news reached David at Ziklag, he was grief-stricken. He tore his clothes in sorrow, fasted until evening, and mourned for both Jonathan and Saul.

In spite of Saul's obsessive hatred of him, David's grief

was genuine. He had refused to raise his hand against the Lord's anointed. In spite of his own destiny, shown when Samuel anointed him to be king, David had not grasped the leadership by removing Saul. Now that Saul lay dead, loyalty still bound David's heart to him. He showed this in the lament he composed for Saul and Jonathan and taught to his men:

Your glory, O Israel, lies slain on your heights.
　　How the mighty have fallen!

Tell it not in Gath,
　　proclaim it not in the streets of Ashkelon,
lest the daughters of the Philistines be glad,
　　lest the daughters of the uncircumcised rejoice.

O mountains of Gilboa,
　　may you have neither dew nor rain,
　　nor fields that yield offerings of grain.
For there the shield of the mighty was defiled,
　　the shield of Saul—no longer rubbed with oil.
From the blood of the slain,
　　from the flesh of the mighty,
the bow of Jonathan did not turn back,
　　the sword of Saul did not return unsatisfied.

Saul and Jonathan—
　　in life they were loved and gracious,
　　and in death they were not parted.
They were swifter than eagles,
　　they were stronger than lions.

O daughters of Israel,
　　weep for Saul,
who clothed you in scarlet and finery,
　　who adorned your garments with ornaments of
　　　gold.

How the mighty have fallen in battle!
   Jonathan lies slain on your heights.
I grieve for you, Jonathan my brother;
   you were very dear to me.
Your love for me was wonderful,
   more wonderful than that of women.

How the mighty have fallen!
   The weapons of war have perished!
                    (II Sam 1:19–27, NIV)

David further underlined his continuing commitment to
Saul by his reaction to the man who brought the news of his
death. An Amalekite brought Saul's crown to David and
claimed responsibility for inflicting the death blow to the
king. David had him executed immediately.

### Patience that Showed Great Maturity of Judgement

When David's grief and anger grew less, he still acted with
a caution that showed that his experience at Ziklag was still
powerful in his memory. 'Shall I go and take control of one
of the towns of Judah?' he asked God, and received an
affirmative answer (II Sam 2:1). Still hesitant, he asked,
'Which one?' When God directed him to Hebron, only then
did he go. When he and his men had settled around Hebron, the elders of Judah, his own tribe, came and asked him
to be their king. Only on their request did he consent and
begin to reign (2:1–4).

   For seven years more David continued to exercise patience. Abner, Saul's former commander-in-chief, took the
prince Ishbosheth to Mahanaim and made him king over
the other eleven tribes of Israel. This rival regime in the

North began to wage war on Judah, but David did no more than defend himself when he was attacked. As David became stronger and his opponents became weaker, Abner decided that he had backed the wrong man and made approaches to David. David listened to him but made it clear that he was still devoted to Saul's family and would not co-operate in a military coup d'état, even with Abner's help. Abner got the message and when he returned to Israel, his words to the elders were:

> For a long time you have wanted David to be your king. Now here is your chance. Remember that the Lord has said, 'I will use my servant David to rescue my people Israel from the Philistines and from all their other enemies.' Abner spoke also to the people of the tribe of Benjamin and then went to Hebron to tell David what the people of Benjamin and of Israel had agreed to do.
>
> (II Sam 3:17–19).

The resulting mass movement took time to materialise but was worth waiting seven years to see. Thousands of fighting men and leaders from every tribe in Israel on both sides of the Jordan descended on Hebron, 'determined to make David king over all Israel.' These clearly represented the rest of the people of Israel, who were 'united in the same purpose' (I Chron 12:38).

David's military ability and earlier popular support demonstrated that, if he had so desired, he could have secured the whole country by force of arms, but he waited to be chosen by the people and confirmed by God. When the time came, he became king not in a bloody battle but in a religious ceremony that confirmed his anointing long ago by Samuel. It was a three-way contract between the man, the people, and God.

## A Political Theory in Advance of its Time

How a person comes to leadership greatly affects what happens thereafter. There are at least seven ways that leaders may come to hold their positions: some become leaders because they volunteer; some are thrust to the front by circumstances; some represent a 'father figure' to followers who desire authoritative direction; some obviously excel beyond the competition; some sense within themselves a divine calling; some represent vested interests; and some are chosen by the majority. David was in advance of his time and certainly more discerning than most men of his years in that although he had several of these characteristics he chose to rise to leadership only by the last alternative. He became king of all Israel by the consent and choice of the people.

David's action was all the more remarkable when compared to the oriental despotism of neighbouring states. He lived in a time when kings ruled autocratically, responsible to no one. The king's word was law. In some neighbouring countries, like Egypt and Assyria, kings laid claim to divinity. Nebuchadnezzar, for example, commanded his subjects to worship a golden image of himself (Dan chapter 3). Surrounded by autocratic monarchs, tempted by Abner's military power, where did David get the idea that he would only consent to become king by the choice of the people?

He took his ideas from the law of God. Long before the Israelites had occupied Canaan, God anticipated that they would one day want a king and made provision for it: 'Make sure that the man you choose to be king is the one whom the Lord has chosen' (Deut 17:15). God's choice came first; the people then ratified it by their choice. The law continues with specific instructions designed to keep the king from

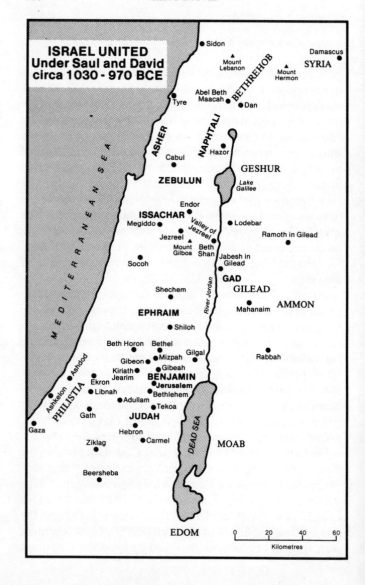

ISRAEL UNITED
Under Saul and David
circa 1030 - 970 BCE

pride: the king was not to have too many horses nor too many wives nor too much gold and silver, and he was to have his own copy of the book of the law and read from it all his life. 'This will keep him from thinking that he is better than his fellow-Israelites and from disobeying the Lord's commands in any way' (Deut 17:20). David, following the law of Moses, established a kind of constitutional monarchy. The people by their common consent chose him to rule for them and voluntarily surrendered certain liberties to him.

The later kings of Judah and Israel did not always adhere to this idea of monarchy. It is significant, however, that the kings who made their mark on the history of the country always returned, either by choice or by the insistence of some prophet, to this mutual three-way contract between the man, the people, and God. It happened to Joash (II Kings chapter 12) and to Hezekiah (II Chron chapter 29). The prophets Elijah, Elisha, Isaiah, Jeremiah, and Amos all preached this covenant relationship between the governed and the governor.

David's subsequent reign, long-lasting and secure in the midst of turmoil in surrounding states, fulfilled the promise of God made through Moses to the man who followed God's pattern for the king: 'Then he will reign for many years, and his descendants will rule Israel for many generations (Deut 17:20).

**A leader is only strong when his immediate subordinates are united.**

*If you act like wild animals, hurting and harming each other, then watch out, or you will completely destroy one another.*
— Paul in Galatians 5:15

# XIII
# Rivalry and Revenge
## II Samuel 1–4

We have gone too fast. David's pathway to the throne of all Israel almost foundered just as it looked most promising. The events were two unwelcome assassinations. The main personalities were Joab and Abner, the two leading soldiers of the administrations David was trying to unite. The issues were family and professional rivalry and two totally different approaches to life.

### The Rivalry

Saul's son Ishbosheth succeeded him on the throne of the rest of Israel, but Abner wielded the real power. Abner was Saul's cousin and commander-in-chief of his military forces (I Sam 14:50–51). He controlled Saul's tribe of Benjamin and knew many of the elders of the other northern tribes. It was through his personal influence that Ishbosheth was made king. By his military acumen he kept him on the throne as a rival to David's newly-declared kingship of Judah (II Sam 2:8–11).

In the civil war between Israel and Judah, at first Abner grew stronger and the king weaker. When Ishbosheth accused Abner of sleeping with one of his father Saul's concubines, Abner's angry outburst cowed Ishbosheth into silence:

> From the very first I have been loyal to the cause of your father Saul, his brothers, and his friends, and I have saved you from being defeated by David; yet today you find fault with me about a woman! The Lord promised David that he would take the kingdom away from Saul and his descendants and would make David king of both Israel and Judah, from one end of the country to the other. Now may God strike me dead if I don't make this come true!
>
> (II Sam 3:8–10)

Clearly, Abner was a man to be reckoned with, a powerful ally and a deadly enemy. When he followed through on his threat and opened talks with David, David responded in ways that attempted to keep in view the good of the whole nation. He asked Abner to consolidate his connection with the house of Saul by restoring to him Michal, Saul's daughter and David's first wife. In addition Abner began to use his political influence to spread the idea among the northern tribes that there might be an advantage in making David king over all Israel.

Abner was a natural professional rival of Joab, David's nephew and a prominent soldier in Judah. In the war between their armies Abner and some of Ishbosheth's men met Joab and some of David's men for talks at the pool of Gibeon. Abner proposed to Joab, 'Let's get some of the young men from each side to fight an armed contest' (II Sam 2:14). Joab agreed, and 12 men from each side lined up with their swords. Before the contest had finished, all 24 died, and the talks erupted into a battle which left 20 of Joab's men and 360 of Abner's men dead.

As the fighting broke up Joab's agile brother Asahel set

off to run down Abner. Not wanting to kill him, Abner twice shouted back to Asahel, '"Stop chasing me! Why force me to kill you? How could I face your brother Joab?" But Asahel would not give up; so Abner, with a backward thrust of his spear, struck him through the belly so that the spear came out at his back' (II Sam 2:22–23). Asahel dropped to the ground dead, and the tribal and professional rivalry between these two powerful men suddenly escalated into a blood feud as Joab swore revenge.

## The Revenge

Abner continued to negotiate with David. When Joab returned from a raiding party and discovered that Abner had come to Hebron and had been allowed to leave under David's guarantee of safe conduct, he confronted David: 'What have you done? Abner came to you—why did you let him go like that? He came here to deceive you and to find out everything you do and everywhere you go. Surely you know that!' (II Sam 3:24–25). Storming out of David's presence, Joab sent a party after Abner and brought him and his men back. Joab personally drew Abner aside and stabbed him in revenge for his brother Asahel. All this was done without the authority and contrary to the wishes of David. It was private revenge under the guise of national security, murder rationalised by unproven accusations of Abner's disloyalty. It was a tragedy the scale of which was clearly revealed by David's response to the murder of Abner.

## Danger of Division

The murder threatened to destroy the rapprochement that

had been taking place at Abner's initiative between David and the leaders of the rest of Israel. Alarm spread where there had been growing friendliness (II Sam 4:1).

David quickly, decisively, and openly dissociated himself from the deed: 'The Lord knows that my subjects and I are completely innocent of the murder of Abner' (II Sam 3:28). He reinforced his words by declaring a period of mourning for Abner and insisted that Joab and his men publicly take part in that. He walked behind the coffin at the funeral and even composed a lament for Abner that deepened the sense of national grief. He fasted the whole day of the burial in spite of suggestions that he might be overdoing it.

David's genuine and public grief saved the day: '[The people] took note of this and were pleased ... All David's people and all the people in Israel understood that the king had no part in the murder of Abner' (3:36, 37).

## Irreparable Loss

'Don't you realize,' said David, 'that this day a great leader in Israel has died?' (3:38). From the beginning of the struggling new monarchy in Israel, Abner had been right-hand man to the king, gaining experience that no one else had ever had the opportunity to acquire. He had been the one to smooth things over and keep the affairs of state operating when the king's black moods incapacitated him. His military prowess was great and nearly indispensable. The influence he commanded with the leaders of so many tribes was all gone now that he was dead. It would take years to replace the loss. His assassination left a great gap. The price the nation had to pay for rivalry and revenge between individuals was unacceptable. David not only lost Abner but for a period had also to distance himself from Joab.

## Compounded Weakness

'Even though I am the king chosen by God, I feel weak today,' David confessed (3:39). Earlier Abner had challenged Joab: 'Do we have to go on fighting for ever? Can't you see that in the end there will be nothing but bitterness?' (II Sam 2:26). The cycle of violence is almost inevitable. Those who take the sword perish by the sword. Destabilisation is perpetuated, and a foundation on which anything lasting can be built is repeatedly removed. David was desperately trying to break that cycle. There is no record of how precisely he was going to do it, but he wanted the nation to be at peace and gain strength. However, Joab's smouldering rage, when it burst into flame and devoured Abner, left everyone weaker, including the king.

## Poisoned Springs

'These sons of Zeruiah are too violent for me,' David asserted (II Sam 3:39). It was the custom in Israel to identify people by linking them with their fathers. David was the son of Jesse. His mother is never named. He himself refers to her only as the handmaiden of the Lord or a godly woman. Very frequently, however, if Joab or either of his brothers Asahel or Abishai are mentioned, they are described as the sons of Zeruiah. The impression is of a mother with a strong personality and a consuming ambition for her sons. Given the fact that she was step-sister to David and he was on the throne, there was ample leverage for her schemes to be pursued, and Joab was her main instrument. It meant, however, that David contended constantly with an alternative agenda and a totally different outlook on life

combatting what he was himself trying to do. Joab was ruth-
less, whereas David wanted always to be conciliatory. Joab
was scheming, where David tried to be open and direct.
Joab was domineering and self-serving, in contrast to
David's desire to be the servant of God and of his people.
Because they grew up together David knew all this, yet to
the end he did not have the will to deal with Joab.


## Indecisive Action

The most David could rise to in the face of Abner's assassination was a very colourful curse: 'May the punishment for
it fall on Joab and all his family! In every generation may
there be some man in his family who has gonorrhoea or a
dreaded skin disease or is fit only to do a woman's work or is
killed in battle or hasn't enough to eat!' (3:29). They were
searing, sizzling words, but they left the problem unsolved.
It would appear that indecision like this was characteristic
of David where members of his own family were concerned. 'Nepotism' or favouritism towards relatives comes
from the Latin word for 'nephew', and Joab was David's
nephew. Nepotism has been the curse of leadership in all
countries at all times where considerations of kinship over-
ride the interests of the state and the common good. It
blocks the way to promotion and service for abler and more
loyal people and remains a debilitating running sore in any
administration. David's was no exception.


## The Second Assassination

The immediate effect was to give an uncertain signal to the
officers in the house of Saul. Two of them would seem to

have interpreted David's inaction as condoning the assassination and proceeded to murder Ishbosheth, Saul's son and king of the rest of Israel, in his bed. They brought his head to David and were executed for their pains, in striking contrast to the leniency shown to Joab (II Sam 4:1–12).

By this tortuous and unfortunate route was cleared David's path to the throne of all Israel, as described in the previous chapter.

**Unity needs shared symbols to give it form and permanence.**

*I saw the Holy City, the new Jerusalem, coming down out of heaven from God, prepared and ready, like a bride dressed to meet her husband. I heard a voice speaking from the throne: 'Now God's home is with mankind! He will live with them and they shall be his people. God himself will be with them, and he will be their God.'*

—John in Revelation 21:2–3

# XIV
# Symbols of Unity

*II Samuel chapters 5–6, I Chronicles chapters 11,
13, 15, 16*

The book of Revelation pictures the New Jerusalem coming out of heaven from God. God dwells there, and the light of his glory shines brighter than the sun. There will be no more death, grief, crying or pain. The people will joyfully worship God and the Lamb. This apocalyptic vision of the New Jerusalem had its origin in the earthly reality established by David, who conquered and built the first Jerusalem. From then on Jerusalem became a symbol of the City of God in contrast to Babylon, the city that was not of God.

### A Gift from God

It began with the capture of Jerusalem. Although the Israelites had occupied the Promised Land for three or four centuries, Jerusalem still remained in the hands of the original inhabitants, the Jebusites. Surrounded on three sides by steep valleys and on the fourth side by natural rocky defences, it seemed an impregnable fortress. 'You will never get in here; even the blind and the crippled could keep you out,' (II Sam 5:8) taunted the Jebusites as David's army massed for the attack. Stung by their taunt, David looked for a way to do the impossible.

Jerusalem was captured when David or some of his men climbed up a water tunnel (5:8). In 1867, Captain Warren visited Jerusalem with other pilgrims. At the Pool of Gihon he spotted a cavity in the dark roof and, being an Alpine climber, returned with a ladder and rope. Edging himself into the gap, he climbed for 40 feet vertically hand over hand, foot over foot through the rock until he entered a narrow passage. He scrambled along on hands and knees into a vault scattered with old bottles and broken earthenware. Seeing a chink of light, he squeezed himself through a crack in the rock and found himself in the centre of Jerusalem. He had discovered David's water tunnel. In 1910, more accurate archaeological investigation revealed that this passage dated from the second millennium BC— well before David's time and without doubt the water shaft penetrated 3,000 years before by David's army.

Frank Slaughter in his novel about David suggests that he went out by night alone and stopped to drink at the spring. When he plunged his head into the water, he heard sound communicated by the water, deduced that there was a passageway, and upon investigation discovered the tunnel. However it was discovered, David challenged his men, promising the position of commander-in-chief of the army to the one who would lead the attack through the water tunnel. Joab accepted the challenge, led the successful surprise attack, and reinstated himself in David's favour.

The impossible had happened. This time it was not military genius, skill, strategy or courage. Instead, Jerusalem was seen as given by God. Psalmist, priest, prophet, prince, and people all believed that God was in the founding of Israel's capital: 'The Lord built his city on the sacred hill,' sang the psalmist: 'more than any other place in Israel he loves the city of Jerusalem' (Ps 87:1). It was no ordinary city, this City of David.

## The Focus of Unity

In addition to the strategic advantage of his new fortress, David made Jerusalem the focus for unifying Israel, for making a nation out of a conglomeration of 12 disparate tribes. David belonged to Judah, the largest of the tribes, and Saul had come from Benjamin. Since both tribes had some claim to the throne, David needed symbols of their unity. Jerusalem stood on the border between Judah and Benjamin, and since it had never been conquered, it belonged to neither of them. In a stroke of political genius David moved his court from Hebron, in Judah, to Jerusalem and made it his new capital city.

The first city of any significance in Israel began to break down the tribal mentality, to transcend the old blood ties and replace them with a new loyalty. As a citizen of Jerusalem, no one was excluded because of background or former allegiance. In Jerusalem everyone was a stranger, and the strangers became fellow-citizens who shared common responsibilities, trials and opportunities.

In establishing Jerusalem as a focus of unity, David created a prototype for the ideal of Christian unity. Paul used the imagery of the city when he welcomed the Ephesian converts into God's family: 'You Gentiles are not foreigners or strangers any longer; you are now fellow-citizens with God's people' (Eph 2:19). In his vision of the New Jerusalem, John pictured the gates of the city always open to the peoples of the world and the kings of the earth moving freely through its streets (Rev 21:24–25). In the concept of 'the city of God' there is no room for any form of Christian tribalism. This ideal had its root in the reality established by David when he conquered and built Jerusalem.

## The Centre of Worship

One of David's first acts in Jerusalem was to try to bring the Ark of the Covenant into the city. Built in the time of Moses, the Ark was an ancient piece of religious furniture symbolising God's presence among his people. It was a box containing the two tablets of the law or the Ten Commandments, and on the lid, called the Mercy Seat, stood two gold cherubim with outstretched wings. God promised to meet with his people there and speak to them from between the cherubim.

In the Promised Land, however, the Ark had never had a permanent home. It was at Shiloh for a long time; then it was captured by the Philistines; subsequently it was returned to a town called Kiriath Jearim. God had promised Moses that he would choose a place for the Ark to dwell, where the people could come and worship (Deut 12:5), and David dared to believe that it might be Jerusalem. 'So David assembled the people of Israel from all over the country, from the Egyptian border in the south to Hamath Pass in the north, in order to bring the Covenant Box from Kiriath Jearim to Jerusalem (I Chron 13:5).

The first attempt ended in disaster. God had given specific instructions that the Ark was always to be carried on the shoulders of men, supported by poles placed through the rings on each corner. No one except the Levites were to carry it, and no one else was permitted to touch it because it was holy. In the flush of victory, David did not follow these instructions. He placed the Ark on an ox-drawn cart and formed a procession of people dancing, singing, and playing instruments. When the oxen began to rock the cart, Uzzah, one of the men in charge, put out his hand to steady it, and God struck him dead. Angry and afraid to take it any further, David left the Ark in the house of a man named Obed Edom.

Three months later, however, when he saw that God had blessed the family of Obed Edom, David was encouraged again to assemble Israel to move the Ark. This time the Levites carried it and played on harps and cymbals. Priests offered sacrifices of bulls and sheep along the way. The people rejoiced and danced as the Ark entered Jerusalem, a symbol of God dwelling with his people, making Jerusalem the Holy City.

### The Heart of the Culture

The city saw great developments in architecture. After capturing the fortress, David lived in it and built a city round it, starting at the place where the land was filled in on the hill. Later King Hiram of Tyre sent a trade mission to supply David with cedar logs, stonemasons and carpenters to build a palace (II Sam 5:9–12). This building programme was to advance even more rapidly under his son Solomon.

The city gave impetus to the output of literature such as the poetry of the Psalms and Song of Solomon, the historical writings of Kings and Chronicles, and soon to the wisdom literature of Proverbs and Ecclesiastes. New musical instruments were invented and used with great choirs in elaborate worship.

David had realised an ideal—a new capital city, replacing tribal rivalry with national unity, and all its developing culture and administrative activity was infused with the presence of God among his people. So he took up his harp and sang this song:

I was glad when they said to me,
   'Let us go to the Lord's house.'
And now we are here,
   standing inside the gates of Jerusalem!

Jerusalem is a city restored
   in beautiful order and harmony.
This is where the tribes come,
   the tribes of Israel,
to give thanks to the Lord
   according to his command.
Here the kings of Israel
   sat to judge their people.

Pray for the peace of Jerusalem:
   'May those who love you prosper.
   May there be peace inside your walls
   and safety in your palaces.'
For the sake of my relatives and friends
   I say to Jerusalem, 'Peace be with you!'

(Ps 122)

**Management is the art of accomplishing things effectively through people.**

*God does not want us to be in disorder but in harmony and peace.*

— Paul in I Corinthians 14:33

# XV
# Effective Administration
*II Samuel 8, 20, 23; I Chronicles 18, 27, 28*

'David ruled over all Israel and made sure that his people were always treated fairly and justly' (II Sam 8:15). After waiting so many years, David finally had the opportunity to use his leadership abilities to administer the new nation of Israel. When he came to the throne he found no effective administrative structure, only a group of loosely connected tribes with no cohesive life. Some movement toward national unity had occurred under Samuel and Saul, but there had been no really sustained effort. In administering Israel he was doing something for the first time. Here David serves as an example not only of the godly person, but also of the effective administrator. In this he followed Moses and took his cue from the books of the law. There Moses, at the founding of the nation, at great length outlined the organisation needed to get the people through the wilderness and into the Promised Land. Now David again illustrates the importance of organisation when, for the first time, they occupied all the territory promised to them.

## The Structure

David first of all secured Israel's borders. By successive

military conquests he surrounded Israel with a ring of sub-servient states: on the east Moab and Ammon, on the south the Ammorites and the Philistines, on the north the Arameans and Syrians. In each conquered state he placed garrisons of soldiers, appointed governors, and wherever possible he drew up treaties and made trade pacts. Not only did tribute from these territories fill his treasury, but this series of buffer states also acted as a cushion between Israel and its greater enemies like Egypt to the south and Assyria to the east.

The structure of David's army was shaped like a pyramid, with his commander-in-chief, Joab, at the top. Next came a group of men of outstanding ability in the art of war known as The Three, followed by a larger group of distinguished soldiers known as The Thirty. A total of 37 fighting men earned a coveted place in this select group, but their achievements are all played down in comparison to the daring feats of The Three. Underneath these famous fighting men David had a mobilised army on call from the people of Israel which he had divided into companies of 1,000 and units of 100. Distinct from this national army, David also maintained a personal bodyguard comprised of Cherethites and Pelethites, probably Aegean peoples, who had very little connection with the mainland of Palestine. This independent unit of highly trained men was untouched by tribal rivalries and remained loyal to David even when he was later faced with Absalom's revolution.

For civil administration David devised a system to smooth the transition from tribe to nation. He divided the country according to population into 12 geographical units from which he expected each month a different group of 24,000 men to be assigned to government service. He retained representatives from the clans and tribes. Whenever an important matter demanded discussion, both the officers of his new administrative units and the old leaders of the tribes would be heard. David recognised the tribe and the tribal leaders, but he recognised too the need for moving from tribal to national administration.

There was also an embryonic civil service. A minister of finance was responsible for the royal treasury and its tribute money collected from surrounding nations. A deputy finance minister oversaw the collection of taxes from the cities, towns, and villages. Under the minister of agriculture one had charge of the vineyards, another of olive and sycamore growing, and a third of the production of olive oil and other products. In the department of animal husbandry David assigned one official to oversee the raising of cattle and camels, another for asses, and a third for sheep and goats. A minister of works, Adoniram, was responsible for the forced labour of prisoners of war in the construction of public buildings and roads. For an emerging nation it made an effective civil service.

To head his administration David formed a cabinet consisting of Joab, the commander-in-chief of the army; Benaiah, the leader of the bodyguard; two priests Zadok and Ahimelech, who had belonged to his company for many years; a recorder called Ahilud, who, following the Egyptian administrative model, kept the records, arranged the king's appointments and served as an officer of public relations; a secretary, who may have been an Egyptian brought in to help organise the palace; Adoniram, the minister of works; and two personal advisors: Ahithophel, called the king's counsellor, and Hushai the Archite, called simply 'the king's friend'. These nine people helped David to move Israel to nationhood.

## The Secret

What made David's administration work? From the very beginning he rewarded ability. Without regard for tribe or place of origin, he looked for men of ability and gave them responsibility over specific areas of the nation's life. Although David's own tribe of Judah comprised about 25% of the total population, David did not give it preferential treatment. Out of 30 men chosen as leaders of his administration, only seven were known to be from Judah. Among the officers of the 12 administrative districts five came from Judah but others came from Ephraim, from Dan, from Naphtali, from Reuben, from Gilead, and from the rival tribe of Benjamin. In fact, in the list of the officers of David's administration nearly all are described by their town of origin rather than by their father's name or by their tribe. The inferences are that David scoured the country for ability and that it didn't matter where he found it. Even if a hamlet didn't merit mention on the map, if he found there a person of demonstrated worth, David would press him into his service.

David also showed appreciation. In the long lists of names of officials in his administration many little details show that David noticed what his men did and what they were. If there was anything to be said to the credit of a man, the recorder inserted it in the text. We know the daring exploits of The Three and many of those of The Thirty (I Chron chapter 11). In the lists of men that came to David just before he was made king of Israel, many little phrases light up the narrative with David's appreciation: men from Judah are described as 'well equipped men, armed with shields and spears', men from Simeon are 'well trained', men from Zebulun are 'loyal and reliable men ready to fight, trained to use all kinds of weapons', leaders from Issachar 'knew what Israel should do and the best time to do it', even men from Ephraim, apparently untested yet in battle are described as 'men famous in their own clans' (chapter 12). If David could find anything distinctive to say, he made sure that the recorder wrote it down. He fostered loyalty by commending all the qualities that they brought to his service.

David's administration succeeded, too, because he was approachable. Although he headed a growing organisation, people could still approach him and have their complaints heard. Nathan could approach him about Bathsheba (II Sam chapter 12); the woman of Tekoa sent by Joab could approach him about Absalom (chapter 14). David personally heard cases that were referred to him from the local courts. David himself consulted people. Before he moved the Ark of the Covenant into Jerusalem, 'King David consulted with all the officers in command of units of a thousand men and units of a hundred men. Then he announced to all the people of Israel, "If you give your approval and if it is the will of the Lord our God, let us send messengers to the rest of our countrymen and to the priests and Levites in their towns, and tell them to assemble here with us"' (I Chron 13:1–2). The assembled people discussed his proposal, 'were pleased with the suggestion and agreed to it' (13:4). It was not government for the sake of government, but government for the people. 'David realised that the Lord had established him as king of Israel and was making his kingdom prosperous for the sake of his people' (I Chron 14:2).

To crown all, David was adaptable and held himself accountable to God. He could change his mind, and he could admit that he was wrong. He made a great mistake in deciding to take a census. No census had been taken of Israel since the time of Numbers, and now David's vanity overcame his wisdom. He wanted to see how many people he had. Joab protested, 'May the Lord make the people of Israel a hundred times more numerous than they are now! Your Majesty, they are all your servants. Why do you want to do this and make the whole nation guilty?' (I Chron 21:3). In his pride, however, David insisted that the census go forward until he realised God's displeasure, admitted his mistake, and stopped the counting. 'I have committed a terrible sin in doing this! Please forgive me. I have acted foolishly' (21:7).

God heard his prayer, stopped the epidemic which had struck the nation as punishment, and gave David a vision of the angel of the Lord, sword drawn in judgement, stopped at the threshing-place of Araunah just before entering Jerusalem. In contrition David raised an altar at that spot, which subsequently became the site of the temple. Unlike most leaders, David could build an altar to God at the place of his error, and then change the direction of his administration. He was conscious of having been placed on his throne by God and he held himself accountable to God.

**To do less for God than you do for yourself shows where your heart is.**

*Jesus said, 'Love the Lord your God with all your heart, with all your soul, and with all your mind. This is the greatest and the most important commandment.'*

— Matthew 22:37, 38

# XVI
# Priorities
*II Samuel 7; I Chronicles 15–17, 22–26, 28*

'King David was settled in his palace, and the Lord kept him safe from all his enemies. Then the king said to the prophet Nathan, "Here I am living in a house built of cedar, but God's Covenant Box is kept in a tent!"' (II Sam 7:1–2). To David it was a principle: he would not do for God less than he would do for himself. He would not do for the house of God less than he would do for his own house. He was building a city, developing a culture, and founding a nation. It was unthinkable to him that the symbol of the presence of God, the Ark of the Covenant, should still have only the trappings of Israel's long-past nomadic existence. When the people were travelling in the wilderness, they too had lived in tents; but now that they lived in houses of stone and cedar, it seemed sacrilegious to leave the symbol of the worship of God two centuries back under a tent. Even though God, through Nathan the prophet, forbade him to build the Temple himself because of the blood of battles on his hands, David still devoted enormous energy and expense to preparing for the temple, to be built by his son Solomon.

## Preparing for the Temple

First David chose and purchased the site for the future Temple—the threshing-place of Araunah, where the angel of the Lord had stayed his hand and spared Jerusalem. When Araunah offered to give the site to David, and his own oxen for a sacrifice, David declined his generous offer: 'No, I will pay you for it. I will not offer to the Lord my God sacrifices that have cost me nothing' (II Sam 24:24).

David then drew up the plans and detailed specifications. He started assembling the required materials—cedar logs from Tyre and Sidon, marble blocks cut by foreign craftsmen, tons of gold and silver and an unlimited supply of bronze and iron. He engaged craftsmen, stonecutters, masons, carpenters and those skilled in all kinds of metal work.

Not content with the preparations made at public expense, David made his own private contribution and challenged his people to do the same: 'Over and above all this that I have provided, I have given silver and gold from my personal property because of my love for God's Temple' (I Chron 29:3).

In a public ceremony David announced that Solomon would build the temple and presented him with the detailed specifications: '"All this"'—he said, finishing his list, '"is contained in the plan written according to the instructions which the Lord himself gave me to carry out"' (28:19).

## The Administrative System for the Temple

David was also the architect of the Temple administration. All the descendants of Aaron were registered and divided

into family groups. In the presence of the king and his officials, the chief priest Zadok drew lots to establish a rota system for burning incense and offering sacrifices as pre-
scribed in the law of Moses. Each family group of priests in
rotation was responsible for serving in the Temple for
about a fortnight each year. So efficiently did David plan
this system that one thousand years later, just before the
birth of John the Baptist, the rota was still working. When
the angel announced to Zechariah that his wife was to have
a son, Zechariah, who belonged to the priestly family of
Abijah—eighth in David's list of 24—was taking his turn in
the daily temple service and had been chosen by lot to burn
incense on the altar (Luke 1:5–8).

David registered all the male Levites also, and devised a
new, comprehensive administrative system to take care of
other Temple functions. These included the care of the
Temple premises; ritual purification; the procurement,
storage and preparation of all the elements used in worship;
security and crowd control; and the collection and disburse-
ment of finances (I Chron 23:28–31).

In addition to those Levites chosen to help the priests in
the temple worship, David assigned others to administrative tasks such as keeping records and settling disputes for
the people of Israel. No detail was too small to be worked
out in David's plan, and no position too unimportant to be
filled by qualified and able people.

### The Temple Music

Four thousand Levites were divided into 24 groups of 166
each and were appointed to 'praise the Lord, using the musical instruments provided by the king for this purpose'
(23:5). At the core of this group were 24 expert musicians

and their families. Trained musicians—288 all skilled on
the harps, lyres, cymbals and trumpets—established a
school of music and drew lots for their duties. They carried
the responsibility for proclaiming God's message through
music and for choosing and training those with the ability to
carry on the music of the house of the Lord.

There is a tradition that in the days of high festival when
all the singers and musicians were in full swing, the Temple
music could on occasions be heard 15 miles away. The system that David had set in place with the help of the
prophets Gad and Nathan for the disciplined but magnifi-
cent worship of God was still remembered and recovered
centuries later by Hezekiah (II Chron 29:25–30).

David is of course best known for the fact that he composed music and words for both musicians and singers. Of
the 150 psalms in the Book of Psalms, 78 bear the title, 'A
Psalm of David', and if we are to believe Athanasius, who
said that the 150 were chosen from a collection of some
3,000 then in use, David's creative production may have
been much higher. Other skilled Levite musicians composed psalms for the Temple worship. One of those praises
God for his Temple and for the king who planned its building, organised its administration and provided for its worship, because he would not do less for God than he would
for himself:

> How I love your Temple, Lord Almighty!
>     How I want to be there!
>     I long to be in the Lord's Temple.
> With my whole being I sing for joy to the living God.
> Even the sparrows have built a nest,
>     and the swallows have their own home;
> they keep their young near your altars,
>     Lord Almighty, my king and my God.
> How happy are those who live in your Temple,

always singing praise to you.

How happy are those whose strength comes from
    you,
  who are eager to make the pilgrimage to Mount
    Zion.
As they pass through the dry valley of Baca,
  it becomes a place of springs;
  the autumn rain fills it with pools.
They grow stronger as they go;
  they will see the God of gods on Zion.

Hear my prayer, Lord God Almighty.
  Listen, O God of Jacob!
Bless our king, O God,
  the king you have chosen.

One day spent in your Temple
  is better than a thousand anywhere else;
I would rather stand at the gate of the house of my
    God
  than live in the homes of the wicked.
The Lord is our protector and glorious king,
  blessing us with kindness and honour.
He does not refuse any good thing
  to those who do what is right.
Lord Almighty, how happy are those who trust in
    you!

(Ps 84)

**It is not your mistakes but what you do with them that determines the kind of person you are.**

*If we confess our sins to God, he will keep his promise and do what is right. He will forgive us our sins and purify us from all our wrongdoing.*

— I John 1:9

# XVII
## Character
*II Samuel 11–12; Psalms 32 and 51*

Soon after David came to power, the moral graph of his life plunged to an all-time low and stayed there for about a year before it began to rise again. It is the story of how he got his eighth wife, Bathsheba, and by her, his son and successor, Solomon.

His first wife was the princess Michal, Saul's daughter. The biblical account says little of her before David became a fugitive. She was given to another for a time and when he got her back, she seemed totally out of sympathy with her husband and gave him no children.

The second was Abigail (see chapter IX). Neither she nor her children became involved in the court intrigues in Jerusalem. Of the next five, we know little more than their names. Apparently David also had some concubines.

The eighth was Bathsheba, the granddaughter of Ahitophel, his most trusted counsellor, and wife of one of the hand-picked officers in his personal bodyguard—Uriah the Hittite. David made love to her, made her pregnant, unsuccessfully attempted to cover up her pregnancy by bringing Uriah home from battle to make him look like the father of the child, sent Uriah back to the front lines carrying sealed orders for his own death, and then made the widowed Bathsheba his wife.

There can be little question that David's wiving tendency was far from being a good thing either for himself or for his kingdom, but the treatment of this final story of its kind in David's life is clearly meant to make several points. Its primary purpose is to indicate that the wise Solomon who succeeded him was a child of love. There is here also a prelude and explanation for the terrible family feuds that raged in and out of the palace. Genealogy, however, is not all of it. Here is an experience of deep moral significance, which when linked with the Psalms that were written as a result, is timeless in its reference and reveals the essential character of the man.

Our method will be to put the factual account together with the parable and denunciation of Nathan the prophet and try to chart the progress of David's soul through his deepest fall and perhaps his most sublime recovery.

### What Sin Is

Over that terrible year David learned the essential nature of sin—that is, to take what belongs to another. After Bathsheba's child had been born, Nathan the Prophet came to David with a parable about two men, one rich in cattle and sheep and lands, the other poor with only one lamb. When a visitor arrived at the rich man's house, instead of using one of his own lambs, the rich man took the poor man's lamb, killed it, and cooked it to feed his guest. Then Nathan made the application. Not content with his seven wives, David had robbed Uriah of his wife.

Almost all sin involves taking what belongs to another: breaking the first commandment to have no other gods robs God of his place; breaking the second commandment not to make graven images robs God of his character;

breaking the third commandment about taking the name of God in vain robs God of his due respect; breaking the fourth commandment about the Sabbath Day robs God of his worship and men of the health of body and mind that comes through observing his day; breaking the fifth about parents robs them of their maintenance and respect; breaking the sixth about killing robs men of their lives; breaking the eighth about stealing robs men of their property; breaking the ninth about false witness robs men of their good name and character; and breaking the tenth about coveting takes away all these things in intent rather than in the act. By the standard of the law of Moses, so much valued by David, Nathan's parable taught him that sin is taking what belongs to another.

In his initial self-righteous response to Nathan's parable, David said that the rich man had no pity for the poor man. He failed to put himself sympathetically in the place of the other who was affected by his action. Then Nathan revealed that David was in fact describing his own lack of regard for Uriah.

Nathan's denunciation also taught David that sin lacks a sense of proportion; it values the present moment rather than the longer consequences. Nathan continued, 'This is what the Lord God of Israel says: "I made you king of Israel and rescued you from Saul. I gave you his kingdom and his wives; I made you king over Israel and Judah. If this had not been enough, I would have given you twice as much. Why, then, have you disobeyed my commands?"' (II Sam 12:7–9). In one night David forgot all that life had already given him, and all that God might yet give him. He failed to be grateful for what he had or realise what he would lose. His whole perspective was momentarily warped.

There was one more thing to learn. Nathan put it crisply. Sin despises God and his Word, and David had ignored

God's Word. Maybe he thought he would be the exception
to the rule. Maybe he thought God would turn a blind eye.
Maybe he thought God did not understand the difficult conditions in his household. Nathan called this attitude by its
true name—contempt for the Almighty.

These were deep lessons for David. He had discovered
that the effects of sin in his private life would spill over into
his public life, and he could not contain the damage.

## What Not to Do with Sin

In the long, dismal year when David tried to ignore his sin,
he learned what not to do in such a case. There was no use
trying to cover up his wrongdoing by stepping up righteousness in other areas. He tried to treat Uriah generously,
granting him leave from the army, entertaining him with
royal hospitality, and urging him to go home to his wife. He
also tried to compensate for his private wrongdoing by his
strictness as a judge of public wrongdoing. David meted out
justice with unerring perception when people came to him
with their unresolved quarrels. When Nathan came to him
with his story of the rich man and the poor man, David
exploded with characteristic anger against the rich man: 'I
swear by the living Lord that the man who did this ought to
die! For having done such a cruel thing, he must pay back
four times as much as he took (12:5–6). David, however,
was just compensating for his own guilt, attempting to direct attention away from himself onto the weaknesses of
others.

It was worse than useless to try and remove the first sin by
committing another. He tried to cover up his adultery first
by deceit and then by murder. He discovered to his conster-
nation that the piling of sin upon sin, once begun, multi-

plied exponentially until it got out of control.

Finally, he learned to his cost not to implicate another in his sin and thus put himself in his power. David's desperate decision to order Uriah into the front lines placed himself in Joab's power. David had reacted with great indignation when Joab had assassinated his rival Abner; now he was asking Joab to do a similar deed for himself: 'Put Uriah in the front line, where the fighting is heaviest, then retreat and let him be killed' (II Sam 11:15). As Joab pocketed that letter with an ironic smile, he must have known that he would never hear about Abner again; he now knew some things about David that David would never want to be made public. The balance of power shifted subtly. David had made himself hostage to his subordinate.


## What To Do with Sin

For the better part of a year David delayed dealing with his sin. He hid behind his rationalisation and compensations. 'When I did not confess my sins, I was worn out from crying all day long. Day and night you punished me, Lord; my strength was completely drained, as moisture is dried up by the summer heat' (Ps 32:3–4). Sin took its toll of David and his capacity to govern.

Not until Nathan cleared away the fog from David's rationalising mind did David recognise his conduct for what it was, give it its name, and admit it as sin: 'I have sinned against the Lord' (II Sam 12:13), David said simply to Nathan. In Psalm 51, written afterwards, he plumbed the depths of agonising penitence:

Wash away all my evil
    and make me clean from my sin!

I recognise my faults;
>    I am always conscious of my sins.
I have sinned against you—only against you—
>    and done what you consider evil.
So you are right in judging me;
>    you are justified in condemning me.
I have been evil from the day I was born;
>    from the time I was conceived, I have been sinful ...
Remove my sin, and I will be clean;
>    wash me, and I will be whiter than snow ...
Create a pure heart in me, O God,
>    and put a new and loyal spirit in me.
Do not banish me from your presence;
>    do not take your holy spirit away from me.
Give me again the joy that comes from your salvation,
>    and make me willing to obey you.

>                                   (Ps 51:2–5, 7, 10–12)

David cast himself on the mercy of God until he felt his broken spirit healed and rejoicing again.

As at Ziklag (see chapter XI) David again showed his willingness to accept the consequences of his actions. When Nathan prophesied that the child born to Bathsheba would die, David fasted and prayed to God to spare the child's life; but when the child did die, David washed himself, worshipped in God's house and returned to the palace to eat. To his officials, who were mystified by his behaviour, David explained, 'I did fast and weep while he was still alive. I thought that the Lord might be merciful to me and not let the child die. But now that he is dead, why should I fast? Could I bring the child back to life? I will some day go to where he is, but he can never come back to me' (II Sam 12:22–23).

In time David arose to live again by the mercy of God. 'Then David comforted his wife Bathsheba. He had intercourse with her, and she bore a son, whom David named Solomon. The Lord loved the boy and commanded the prophet Nathan to name the boy Jedidiah [Beloved of the Lord], because the Lord loved him' (12:24–25). The story of David and Bathsheba, then, has at least two endings. One is positive. Solomon was blessed by God with wisdom because he was successor to David's throne. In the very relationship where David had sinned, and in response to his penitence, the mercy of God was shown.

On the other hand, family feuds plagued the rest of David's life, especially in the sons, who were far from knowing David's God. David himself had seen the end of his long history of poorly controlled passion. The world relives his story with only a limited understanding of its meaning, but his eighth wife appears on the first page of the New Testament as one of the forebears of Jesus the Messiah and Saviour of the world.

**When our worst enemies are from our own families, it says something about the quality of our lives.**

*If a man does not know how to manage his own family, how can he take care of the church of God?*

— I Timothy 3:15

# XVIII
# Family and Business
*II Samuel 5:13–16; II Samuel 13–15; I Kings 1–2*

David had eight wives whose names we know, plus a number of concubines whose names and number we do not know. He had 19 children whose names we know, and presumably others of whom we know nothing. Tamar, the daughter of his fourth wife, was violated by Amnon, the son of his third wife. Absalom, the brother of Tamar, openly murdered his half-brother Amnon at a feast with all the royal sons present. Absalom thereafter spent three years in self-imposed exile at the home of his mother's parents.

After that time he was brought back to the capital through the intervention of Joab, the commander-in-chief of the army, to spend two more years without seeing his father's face. Discontented with this, he forced Joab's hand to act again and was restored to the palace, but no sooner had he returned than he began to plot and carry through a revolution that sent his father into exile. Eventually Absalom was killed by his former advocate Joab, against David's orders, as he hung by the hair from a branch of a tree.

In turn, when David was about to die, Adonijah, the son of his fifth wife, tried to effect a coup, but David put it down in favour of Solomon, the son of his eighth wife, a favourite

# DAVID'S FAMILY TREE

Based on a diagram in the Lion Handbook to the Bible, and used by permission.

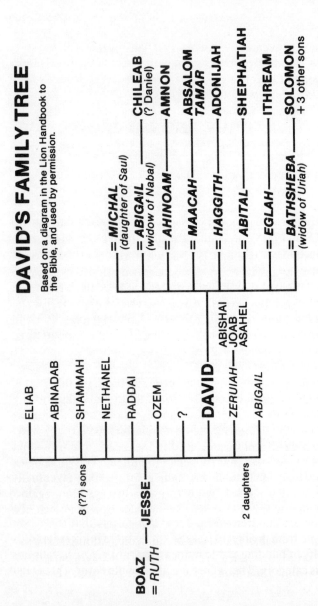

David had several other sons and at least one daughter, Tamar.

son who eventually had his rival half-brother killed.

A sad story of court intrigue, this saga of the royal family of one of history's great kings underscores a leader's need to keep his own house in order.

## Care After a Bad Start

As we saw in chapter I, David had grown up an unwanted or at least an unappreciated child in a divided home. He had two sisters, Zeruiah and Abigail (I Chron 2:16), who were also daughters of Nahash, the king of the Ammonites (II Sam 17:25), and thus apparently half-sisters of David by a second marriage. We do not know whether the mother of these two girls was the wife, the widow, or the concubine of Nahash. We do not know whether Jesse took her as a second wife or as his only wife after his first wife's death. We do not know of which wife David was son. We do know, however, that he was the youngest son and somewhat resented by the older brothers (I Sam chapters 16–17), and the inference is that he may have been a late child by Jesse's second marriage. In spite of the gaps in our information, an unhappy start for David emerges in that household in Bethlehem.

Trouble often runs in families. The laws of heredity and environment combine to perpetuate both the strengths and the weaknesses of the line. In the Decalogue it is said that God punishes evildoers down to the third and fourth generation (Deut 5:9). Contemporary social science interprets the matter differently but draws the same conclusion about problem children and homes. It confirms that those who come from divided or broken homes often find greater difficulty in building stable homes themselves. David falls into this category. The aggressive, passionate nature that David

developed in his divided family made him one of the
world's great kings but one of the world's worst fathers. He
failed to counter the adverse effects of his family
background as he created his own home, and he failed to
order his home to avoid perpetuating the same adverse
effects on the next generation. The cycle of trouble ran full
circle and began again in the lives of his children.

## The Necessity of Complete Obedience

Deuteronomy chapter 17 had laid down the requirements
for Israel's king, and with one exception David followed
them rigorously: 'The king is not to have many wives, because this would make him turn away from the Lord' (Deut
17:17). David was in fact a polygamist.

The biblical position regarding polygamy is ambiguous.
To say that the Old Testament allows polygamy is to speak
only half the truth. Adam, Cain, Noah and his three sons—
all seem to have had only one wife. This is the beginning to
which Jesus refers when he speaks to the Pharisees about
divorce, saying, 'It was not like that at the time of creation'
(Matt 19:8). In the beginning monogamy, or one man
married to one wife, was the ideal. In the less godly line described in Genesis, six generations removed from Cain,
Lamech started the process by taking two wives. He is the
first polygamist mentioned in Scripture.

Although the law of Moses discourages rather than bans
having more than one wife, the Old Testament gives no picture of contented polygamy. Invariably the story throbs
with pain and unhappiness. Abraham had several wives
whose unhappy story ended with tragic consequences, still
multiplied to this day in the hatred between Jew and Arab.
Jacob had several wives, breeding disunity and trouble in his

home and in his descendants. Elkanah had two wives, who filled his home with bitter rivalry (I Sam 1:1–8). In Matthew 19:8 Jesus emphasises that a plurality of wives was not God's intention for mankind: 'It was not like that at the creation.'

David's case is one of the unhappiest. He seems not to know what he wanted or what he needed in a wife, and had little opportunity to learn. He moved his attentions from one wife to another, multiplying his harem. Although he knew that he would become king, he married three wives before his coronation. After his succession to the throne he added five wives, plus several concubines. David's failure in this part of the Law produced a family story of pain and tragedy. 'What boots it at one gate to make defence,' wrote Milton in *Samson Agonistes*, 'and at another to let in the foe?'

## The Paralysing Effect of Guilt

David's family troubles are traced to what happened in the case of Bathsheba. In contrast to the legal marriages that preceded hers, David married Bathsheba after committing adultery, deceitfully trying to make Uriah seem to be the father, and finally ordering his death by a ruse on the battlefield. Nathan prophesied the consequences. The Lord said, 'Now, in every generation some of your descendants will die a violent death because you have disobeyed me and have taken Uriah's wife. I swear to you that I will cause someone from your own family to bring trouble on you' (II Sam 12:10–11). The Prophet was confirming that the laws of heredity and environment would operate naturally under God and that David, paralysed by his guilt and bad example, would be powerless to stop them.

When David heard, therefore, that Amnon had violated

his step-sister Tamar, he was furious but took no disciplinary action (13:21). What could he do? He had done the same to Bathsheba. When Absalom plied Amnon with drink, murdered him, and fled into voluntary exile, David left him there and did nothing, either when he was in exile or when he returned. What could he do? He had done the same to Uriah. What could David say during the revolution when Absalom made love to his concubines on the roof of the palace in the sight of all Israel? Was it strange that Adonijah, having failed in his attempted coup, went pleading to Solomon to be given his father's latest but untouched concubine? It was not surprising that Solomon should have such an extensive harem, when he was brought up in such a home with such a father as David.

David apparently ran a home where discipline was nonexistent. He had never reprimanded Adonijah about anything (I Kings 1:6), and that statement seems true of all the children. No doubt, many factors inhibited David's discipline—an absence of discipline in his father's household, his desire to please his wives, or his business as king that kept him away in battle and preoccupied him with affairs of state while at home. Mostly, however, David had nothing to say because of his own example of ruinous behaviour. Nowhere does guilt paralyse discipline and nullify words so completely as in the home. Although his sin was pronounced forgiven, the tragic effects of his disobedience continued to be experienced in his family for years to come.

Not unexpectedly, the problems arose from the firstborn children of his earlier wives, who seemed to themselves (in turn) to have some claim to the succession. There were some exceptions, however, even among them. Chileab his second son never became a pretender to the throne even after Amnon, his first-born, was murdered.

Perhaps the sagacity of his mother Abigail prevailed in her small corner of the royal household.

Bathsheba was also different. Nathan the Prophet, who had confronted David with his sin against her and her former husband and had confirmed God's forgiveness of David and his love for Solomon, had to prompt her to remind the king of his promise (I Kings 1:11–40). She, with her four sons (I Chron 3:4), seem to have stayed away from palace politics and eventually found a place in the royal line of the Messiah (Matt 1:6), the ultimate stamp of acceptance and sign of God's grace triumphing in a family with such a poor start to its formation.

**People who have a true view of themselves before God cannot be hurt by what others say of them.**

*What credit is there if you endure the beatings you deserve for having done wrong? But if you endure suffering even when you have done right, God will bless you for it. It was to this that God called you, for Christ ... left you an example, so that you would follow in his steps ... when he suffered, he did not threaten, but placed his hopes in God, the righteous Judge.*

— I Peter 2:20, 21, 23

# XIX
# Facing Disaster
*II Samuel chapters 14–17; Psalm 3*

Trouble in his family plagued David's public career, and Absalom was its focus. Handsome, popular, undisciplined and ambitious, he found events smiling on him in a macabre sort of way. Incest with his sister Tamar provided him with the excuse to remove Amnon, David's first-born, from the scene. An unholy alliance with Joab, the ingratiating commander-in-chief of the army, that served both their interests restored him from banishment but only partly to the royal favour. The brooding inactivity of his father provided a public foil for his flair and flamboyant style and increased his rating in the popularity polls of the day, till he was ready to stage his *coup d'état*. When he raised his standard in Hebron, people flocked to him, and soon they were ready to march on Jerusalem.

The significance of Absalom's revolution, however, lies not in the crisis that faced David but in the way that David faced the crisis. Most leaders in David's situation would have reacted to the revolution with violence or anger or fear. Most would have searched for convenient scapegoats to punish like David's counsellor Ahithophel or the soldiers who deserted to support Absalom. Instead David perceived the reasons behind this power struggle and reacted with unusual meekness. David knew that the ultimate

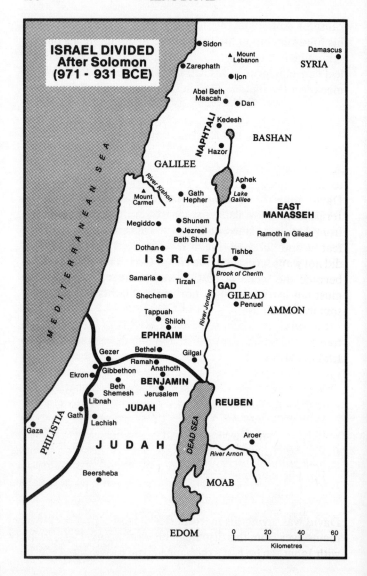

ISRAEL DIVIDED
After Solomon
(971 - 931 BCE)

cause of Absalom's revolution lay not in the fickleness of his followers but in his own failure to discipline his family. Although he had repented, he could see and accept the logical consequences of his actions. He resolved to bear with meekness the hand of God in what was now happening.

## He Did Not Implicate Others

As Absalom's strength increased in Hebron, David moved to keep innocent people from becoming involved. 'So David said to all his officials who were with him in Jerusalem, "We must get away at once if we want to escape from Absalom! Hurry! Or else he will soon be here and defeat us and kill everyone in the city!"' (II Sam 15:14). He did not want Jerusalem, the city of God that he had built, to become the scene of battle. Any recovery of his throne must not involve the city nor its inhabitants when he personally was guilty.

Likewise, as he moved out from the city he offered to free his personal bodyguard, the 600 mercenaries led by Ittai the Gittite:

> Why are you going with us? Go back and stay with the new king. You are a foreigner, a refugee away from your own country. You have lived here only a short time, so why should I make you wander round with me? I don't even know where I'm going. Go back and take your fellow-countrymen with you—and may the Lord be kind and faithful to you.
>
> (15:19–20)

David was giving his mercenaries a chance to disentangle themselves from this dispute in his own family. Early in life with Jonathan he had experienced true friendship. Now he was willing to let his friends go rather than involve them in the consequences of his own misdeeds. The allegiance of Ittai's soldiers had been bought with money, but they stayed out of respect and devotion: 'I swear to you in the Lord's name that I will always go with you wherever you go, even if it means death,' said Ittai (15:21).

## He Refused to Manipulate God

At a deeper level David refused to try and manipulate God to get him out of his difficulty. As David's followers left Jerusalem, Zadok the priest stood at the gate with the Levites carrying the Ark of the Covenant, the symbol of God's presence. David had brought the Ark into the city with great ceremony and enthusiasm, making Jerusalem the holy city: he had brought God into the civic affairs of his capital. Now that David was leaving, the priests decided that he had a right to take the Ark with him. David, however, remembered the battle of Shiloh, where the Israelites had tried to manipulate God by carrying the Ark of the Covenant into battle against the Philistines. Instead of bringing victory, the Ark had been captured and the Israelites defeated. The nation learned then that they could not, with the physical symbol, manipulate God. Instead they had to correct what displeased God.

David's experience taught him that he had forfeited any claim on God, and he refused to try to use the Almighty for his own purposes. He told Zadok, 'Take the Covenant Box back to the city. If the Lord is pleased with me, some day he will let me come back to see it and the place where it stays. But if he isn't pleased with me—well, then, let him do to me what he wishes' (15:25–26). Like Jesus, his greater son, who faced his death and refused to call down legions of angels to deliver him, David did not try to use God.


## He Hoped in God's Mercy

Though he made no demands on God, though he prepared for the worst that could befall him, knowing that it would be no worse than he deserved, yet David still hoped that God might yet find a way to be merciful. When he heard that Ahithophel had joined Absalom's revolution, he prayed 'Please, Lord, turn Ahithophel's advice into nonsense!' (15:31).

Ahithophel and David had been life-long friends and companions. David so respected Ahithophel's judgement that he made him his principal adviser. He did nothing without consulting him and repeatedly the wisdom and judgement of this man forwarded the interests of David's throne. But Ahithophel had a granddaughter named Bathsheba, and after David's adultery with her Ahithophel turned on David, left the court and returned to his ancestral town of Giloh. When Absalom organised his revolution, he made a bid for the political skill of Ahithophel, confident that his bitterness and disillusionment with David would bring him into the conspiracy. When the news reached David that Ahithophel had gone with Absalom, he could only turn to prayer and hope that God in his mercy would spare him from Ahithophel's revenge.

David's second adviser Hushai remained faithful to the king. He sent him back to Jerusalem to Absalom, hoping that God would use Hushai's loyalty to counter Ahithophel's bitterness. With his two prime political advisers in the rebel court of his son, David left the outcome to God—either chastisement through Ahithophel or mercy through Hushai.

David wrote this psalm as he ran from Absalom:

I have so many enemies, Lord,
    so many who turn against me!
They talk about me and say,
    'God will not help him.'

But you, O Lord, are always my shield from danger;
    you give me victory
    and restore my courage.
I call to the Lord for help,
    and from his sacred hill he answers me.

I lie down and sleep,
    and all night long the Lord protects me.
I am not afraid of the thousands of enemies
    who surround me on every side.

Come, Lord! Save me, my God!
You punish all my enemies
    and leave them powerless to harm me.
Victory comes from the Lord—
    may he bless his people.

                                                    (Psalm 3)

Even in the face of revolution occasioned in part by his own
actions, David hoped in God.


### He Knew Himself

As David was leaving Jerusalem he met a relative of Saul
named Shimei. He had nursed bitterness and resentment
against David through all the years of his reign and now
pelted David's troops with clods and curses: 'Get out! Get
out! Murderer! Criminal! You took Saul's kingdom, and

now the Lord is punishing you for murdering so many of
Saul's family. The Lord has given the kingdom to your son
Absalom, and you are ruined, you murderer!' (II Sam
16:7–8).

Abishai asked whether he should go over and take
Shimei's head off. David refused. He knew that Shimei's
accusations were untrue. He had scrupulously treated Saul
and all his family with honour and respect. In other
respects, however, he knew his sins to be worse than anyone could describe. Whatever people chose to believe or to
say behind his back made little difference:

> If he curses me because the Lord told him to, who has
> the right to ask why he does it? ... My own son is try-
> ing to kill me; so why should you be surprised at this
> Benjaminite? The Lord told him to curse; so leave
> him alone and let him do it. Perhaps the Lord will
> notice my misery and give me some blessing to take
> the place of his curse.
>
> (16:10–12)

David had the protection of a broken and contrite heart,
which gave him security in God.


## He Was Not Vindictive

Absalom entered Jerusalem, stole his father's concubines,
amassed an army and marched out to fight against the old
king's loyal forces. As they moved into battle positions,
David gave explicit instructions to his captains for his sake
to deal gently with Absalom. He was not vindictive. He
did not call down the wrath of God on his rebel son. He
knew only grief to see him ranged against him (see chapter
XX).

In his younger days David had been tempted to be vindictive. He had set out in anger to destroy Nabal and all his
household over a small matter of a few roasted sheep.
Abigail had saved him from that, and he had learned his
lesson well. He did not rejoice in the unsought death of his
rival but seemed to hope to the end that Absalom would
change.

In the face of possible disaster, David's character showed
through. All his previous experiences came to his aid, and
he displayed that meekness that Jesus said inherits the
earth.

**Success is a greater test of a person than failure.**

*Jesus said, 'Love your enemies, do good to those who hate you, bless those who curse you, and pray for those who ill-treat you.'*

— Luke 6:27–28

# XX
# Magnanimity
*II Samuel Chapters 18–19*

What a man does when he is down, when he faces defeat, displays the kind of man he is. An even greater test of character is what a man does when he is up, in the flush of victory.

In Absalom's revolution David faced both tests. He was ousted from the capital in the *coup d'état* led by his son. He regrouped his men under the officers who remained loyal and eventually defeated Absalom's army in the forests of Ephraim. David then faced the more severe test. Could he suffer without bitterness?

### Loving Enemies

It began even before the battle. Absalom, the rebel, was to be spared (II Sam 18:5). Afterwards messengers ran to David with news of the battle. 'Is the young man Absalom safe?' (18:29, 32), was his only question. When the battle had been won and Absalom killed by Joab, David felt only grief: 'O my son! My son Absalom! Absalom, my son! If only I had died in your place, my son! Absalom, my son!' (18:33). Unable to understand how an enemy could be loved, Joab complained about

David's sorrow: 'You oppose those who love you and support those who hate you! You have made it clear that your
officers and men mean nothing to you. I can see that you
would be quite happy if Absalom were alive today and all of
us were dead' (II Sam 19:6). His complaint was exagger-
ated, but he accurately gauged the extent to which David
wanted reconciliation. He never ceased to love his
enemy, and the token was the fact that he dismissed Joab
from his post and found a new commander-in-chief.


## Doing Good to Those Who Hate You

The Israelites who had backed Absalom fled to their homes
after the battle. David again moved to overcome evil with
good. He did not rush back to Jerusalem or seek revenge on
the leaders of the rebellion. Instead he fell back on his principle of rule by the consent of the people. When he heard
that people throughout the country were saying, 'Why
doesn't somebody try to bring King David back?' (19:10),
he sent a message to the tribe of Judah, to the very centre of
the rebellion in Hebron: 'Why should you be the last to help
bring the king back to his palace? You are my relatives, my
own flesh and blood' (19:11–12). Instead of confrontation,
David offered them a chance to redeem themselves; instead of reprisals, he offered friendship. He still called
them brothers. He promoted Amasa, who had commanded
Absalom's army: 'You are my relative. From now on I
am putting you in charge of the army in place of Joab'
(19:13).

When the northern tribes and the tribe of Judah started
quarrelling over who had remained more loyal to David
(19:40–43) and when a Benjaminite named Sheba led
another abortive rebellion against David (II Sam 20:1–22)

based on the old tribal rivalry between Judah and Benjamin, David wanted only the restoration of order with the minimum loss of life.


## Blessing Those Who Curse

On his way back to Jerusalem, David's old 'friend' Shimei arrived, bringing with him a thousand men from the tribe of Benjamin. No longer cursing the king, he fell on his face in front of David:

> 'Your Majesty, please forget the wrong I did that day you left Jerusalem. Don't hold it against me or think about it any more. I know, sir, that I have sinned, and this is why I am the first one from the northern tribes to come and meet Your Majesty today.'
>
> (II Sam 19:19–20)

Abishai urged execution, but again David chose magnanimity. He rebuked Abishai and forgave Shimei (19:23). He wanted this to be a day of national reconciliation and spoke mildly and kindly to the one who cursed him in his misfortune.

Such were the approaches David used to consolidate his restoration to the throne. He pursued the way of peace. Political madness? Impractical ethics for public life? Perhaps. But in his handling of this tragic rebellion, David simply anticipated the way of his even greater descendant who taught, 'Love your enemies, do good to those who hate you, bless those who curse you' (Luke 6:27). Jesus added, 'Pray for those who ill-treat you.' There are no such prayers in this part of II Samuel, but there are in the Psalms of David. There he struggled in the presence of God with his vindictiveness and showed how great a fight it was to behave as he did in this instance and how much prayer was essential in the process.

**Leave the world better than you found it.**

*The time is here for me to leave this life. I have done my best in the race, I have run the full distance, and I have kept the faith. And now there is waiting for me the victory prize of being put right with God, the prize which the Lord, the righteous judge, will give me on that Day—and not only to me but to all who wait with love for him to appear.*

— II Timothy 4:6–8

# XXI
# Leaving a Legacy
*II Samuel 23:1–7; I Kings 1–2; I Chronicles 28–29*

The turbulent, sometimes chequered, yet eminently successful career of David came to an end after forty years of ruling a united Israel as its first king. Death, however, is never just an end. It is the passing on of a heritage and the leaving of a legacy. This is often formalised by drawing up a last will and testament, bequeathing lands and money, movable and immovable property. There is much less control over the intangible bequests passed on to others. While the Bible does not record David's last will and testament, it does give ample evidence of the intangible legacy that David passed on to Solomon.

## A Kingdom and a Mission

David bequeathed to Solomon a prosperous kingdom, efficiently organised and effectively administered. From the River Euphrates to Philistia and the Egyptian border subject nations paid him tribute, and the people of Judah and Israel, as numerous as grains of sand on the seashore, grew their grapevines and fig trees in peace. Building on the foundation of his father's reign, Solomon reorganised the 12 administrative districts to achieve a more efficient civil service and lived peacefully in wealth and splendour and wisdom that dazzled even the Queen of Sheba.

Much more than the palace of cedar and marble, the treasury of silver and gold, the stores of olive oil and wheat and the stables of chariots and horses, however, David bequeathed to Solomon a purpose and a mission: 'You must realise that the Lord has chosen you to build his holy Temple. Now do it—and do it with determination' (I Chron 28:10). The great contribution of Solomon's reign to Israel was his life's work of building the Temple (I Kings chapters 5–8). David spent the latter half of his reign drawing up the plans and gathering the materials, but much more than the tons of bronze and iron, the gold and silver and precious stones, the quantities of marble and timber, David bequeathed to Solomon a sense of purpose and a mission. Building the Temple symbolised his devotion to God—an expression of love, a long overdue righting of the inadequate provision for the worship of God. Building the Temple symbolised obedience to God's law. 'The Lord said to me, "Your son Solomon is the one who will build my Temple. I have chosen him to be my son, and I will be his father. I will make his kingdom last for ever if he continues to obey carefully all my laws and commands as he does now"' (28:6–7). David left Solomon his life's work.

## Unfinished Business

Every leader, no matter how good, inevitably leaves behind a legacy of mistakes to be rectified, omissions to be cleared up and poor examples to be counteracted by those who take up where he leaves off. David was no exception. In his last instructions to Solomon David listed a number of problems with which he would have to deal.

There were scores to settle. David had never punished Joab after he murdered Abner; he also killed Amasa, whom David had tried to make commander-in-chief after Joab had disobeyed the royal order to spare Absalom. David's own order to Joab to kill Uriah had effectively prevented him from punishing Joab. Now Solomon had to do the job: 'He killed innocent men and now I bear the responsiblity for what he did, and I suffer the consequences. You know what to do; you must not let him die a natural death' (I Kings 2:5–6). Then there was Shimei, who had cursed the king but whom David had reprieved: 'I gave him my solemn promise in the name of the Lord that I would not have him killed. But you must not let him go unpunished' (2:8–9).

There were omissions to rectify. David felt that he had not rewarded Barzillai enough for his kindness and provisions when David was fleeing from Absalom (2:7).

There were problems inevitably springing from David's neglect of his sons. He had never disciplined Adonijah (I Kings 1:6), and at the very moment when David proclaimed Solomon king, Adonijah, supported by Joab and Abiathar the priest, were gathering support for a *coup d'état*. They would have to be punished.

Perhaps the most difficult legacy for Solomon to counteract was David's bequest of his bad example in breaking the law of Moses that forbade a king from marrying many wives, lest he turn away from the Lord. David had married eight wives and maintained at least ten concubines. Solomon married seven hundred princesses and kept three hundred concubines (I Kings 11:3). Many of them seduced him to worship other gods.

Joab, Shimei, Barzillai, Adonijah, Abiathar, too many wives and too many concubines—all these formed David's bequest of mistakes in judgement for Solomon to correct.

## A Confirmed Covenant

The greatest gift that David handed on not only to
Solomon, but to all his successors, has come to be known as
the Davidic covenant. David instructed Solomon from his
deathbed:

> Obey all his laws and commands, as written in the
> Law of Moses, so that wherever you go you may
> prosper in everything you do. If you obey him, the
> Lord will keep the promise he made when he told me
> that my descendants would rule Israel as long as they
> were careful to obey his commands faithfully with all
> their heart and soul.
>
> (I Kings 2:2–4)

This conditional covenant depended on Solomon's obedience, but it was secured by God's promise. God had been
faithful to David when he defended his father's sheep from
the lion and the bear; faithful when he confronted Goliath
with sling and stone; faithful when he ran from Saul's murderous spear and lived like an outlaw in the desert hills and
caves; faithful when the men of Judah and Israel had made
him king at Hebron; faithful when his army had captured
Jerusalem and he had united the nation in the Holy City;
faithful even when David had violated Bathsheba and suffered the punishment of Absalom's revolution. Confident
now that the God who had been faithful to him all his life
long would be faithful also to his descendants, David for the
final time burst into poetic song to utter his last words:

> The spirit of the lord speaks through me;
>     his message is on my lips.
> The God of Israel has spoken;

the protector of Israel said to me:
'The king who rules with justice,
    who rules in obedience to God,
is like the sun shining on a cloudless dawn,
    the sun that makes the grass sparkle after rain.

And that is how God will bless my descendants,
    because he has made an eternal covenant with me,
    an agreement that will not be broken,
    a promise that will not be changed.
That is all I desire;
    that will be my victory,
    and God will surely bring it about.

(II Sam 23:2–5)

# Epilogue

# Leadership
# and a People's Potential

To Abraham God promised that the whole land of
Caanan would belong to his descendants for ever. As
the Israelites prepared to enter that Promised Land, Moses
had a vision of a nation that stretched from the Red Sea to
the Mediterranean, from the Sinai desert across to the
River Euphrates. Only once, however, during the long
history of God's people did this dream become reality: for
almost a hundred years under the leadership of David, the
first king of all Israel, and under his son Solomon, Israel
reached its potential.

How did this loose federation of tribes subservient to
neighbouring states become Greater Israel, one nation,
never of the same extent or glory before or since? Israel
reached its great potential because its leader reached his. In
the secret of David's success lies also the secret of Greater
Israel.

David early discovered that the first principle of successful leadership was to *know his calling*. While still a teenage
boy herding sheep, David had been anointed king over Israel by the prophet Samuel. God had chosen him, and
David never forgot his calling, not when his older brothers
in Saul's army scorned him, not when Saul banished him
from the palace, not even when his years as an outlaw made

his dream seem remote. David consistently behaved with the conviction that one day he would rule. He did not feel he had to kill Saul; he waited patiently until he received confirmation from the people of Judah and Israel in God's time.

The second principle of his successful leadership was to *limit his field*. David was an 'all-rounder'. He proved his military genius from the moment that Saul made him a commander after the death of Goliath. He effectively administered the civil and ecclesiastical government of Israel, established a civil service and organised the building of public works. He composed 78 psalms for worship, and accompanied them on his harp. He had magnetism and charm and the charisma that attracted people to him and moved them to follow him. Nevertheless, he learned to limit his field. When his men urged him to stay out of the battle and protect his life, David delegated the command of his forces to Joab and Abishai. When God refused to let David build His Temple because of the blood of war on his hands, David contented himself with gathering the gold and silver, stone and cedar, and delegated the job to Solomon. God always limits what he asks any leader to do, and the leader who tries to hold on to responsibility greater than that intended for him inevitably fails to achieve his potential.

The third principle was to *relate well to others*. Nowhere in the Bible do more names of people appear than in the history of David. We know the names of his military leaders, his commander-in-chief, The Three, The Thirty, the captains of thousands, men in his bodyguard. We know the names of his ministers, religious personnel and his personal advisers. Why do we know all these people? They were all important to David. He knew what each of his people should be doing, and he praised them when they did well.

David inspired devotion and loyalty because he related well to his people.

The fourth need for successful leadership was to *develop his character*. Only the leader who knows and understands himself can motivate others. In the Psalms David left a record of his self-discovery—his loves, his hates, his disappointments, his complaints, his depressions and his ecstasies. In the Psalms one sees why David was 'a man after God's own heart'. He was far from perfect, but he was honest with himself and with God. He had serious falls—but even when he learned the hard way he grew in character and developed spiritually.

Healthy self-criticism alone, however, does not develop character. The leader who would reach his potential must also have a positive point of reference. David found his delight in God's law. As he meditated on its wisdom, he slowly experienced the healing and resolution of the conflicts in his personality. The psalms show this to be his secret and in turn tell the story of his nation's rise to its potential.

> The law of the Lord is perfect;
>     it gives new strength.
> The commands of the Lord are trustworthy,
>     giving wisdom to those who lack it.
> The laws of the Lord are right,
>     and those who obey them are happy.
> The commands of the Lord are just
>     and give understanding to the mind.
> Reverence for the Lord is good;
>     it will continue for ever.
> The judgements of the Lord are just;
>     they are always fair.
> They are more desirable than the finest gold;
>     they are sweeter than the purest honey.

They give knowledge to me, your servant;
  I am rewarded for obeying them.

                            (Psalm 19:7–11)

# What Is World Vision?

World Vision is a major Christian relief and development agency, founded over 35 years ago. World Vision now helps the hungry, the homeless, the sick and the poor in over 80 countries worldwide.

World Vision is international, interdenominational and has no political affiliation, working wherever possible through local churches and community leaders in close co-operation with the United Nations and other international relief agencies.

Childcare sponsorship is an important part of World Vision's Christian work. Over 400,000 children are currently being cared for in over 3,500 projects.

Sponsors in Europe and around the world are helping thousands of needy children by supplying food, clothing, medical care and schooling. These children usually live with their families although some are in schools or homes. Development and training are usually offered to the communities where the sponsored children live so that whole families can become self-reliant.

World Vision is able to respond with immediate and appropriate relief in crisis situations such as famines, floods, earthquakes and wars. Hundreds of thousands have been saved in Africa through feeding and medical centres. Other projects include cyclone relief for Bangladesh, relief work in Lebanon and medical assistance for Kampuchea.

Over 500 community development projects in 50 countries are helping people to help themselves towards a healthier and more stable future. These projects include agricultural and vocational training, improvements in health care and nutrition (especially for mothers and babies), instruction in hygiene, literacy classes for children and adults, development of clean water supplies and village leadership training.

World Vision's approach to aid is integrated in the sense

that we believe in helping every aspect of a person's life and needs. We also help Christian leaders throughout the world to become more effective in their ministry and assist local churches in many lands with their work.

If you would like more information about the work of World Vision, please contact one of the offices listed below:

World Vision of Britain
Dychurch House
8 Abington Street
Northampton
NN1 2AJ, United Kingdom
Tel: 0604 22964

World Vision of Australia
Box 399–C, G P O
Melbourne, 3001 Victoria
Australia
Tel: 3 699 8522

World Vision Deutschland
Postfach 1848
Adenauerallee 32
D–6370 Oberursel
West Germany
Tel: 6171 56074/5/6/7

World Vision International
Christliches Hilfswerk
Mariahilferstr 10/10
A-1070 Wien
Austria
Tel: 222–961 333/366

World Vision International
Christliches Hilfswerk
Badenserstr 87
CH-8004 Zürich
Switzerland
Tel: 1–241 7222

World Vision of Ireland
17 Percy Place
Dublin 4
Eire
Tel: 01 606 058

World Vision Singapore
Maxwell Rd
PO Box 2878
Singapore 9048
Tel: 224–8037/7419

Suomen World Vision
Kalevankatu 14 C 13
00100 Helsinki 10
Finland
Tel: 90 603422

World Vision of New Zealand
PO Box 1923
Auckland
New Zealand
Tel: 9 770 879

Stichting World
Vision Nederland
Postbus 818
3800 AV Amersfoort
The Netherlands
Tel: 33 10041

World Vision Canada
6630 Turner Valley Rd
Mississauga, Ontario
Canada L5N 2S4
Tel: 416 821 3030

World Vision United States
919 West Huntington Drive
Monrovia
CA 91016
USA
Tel: 818 303 8811

World Vision of Hong Kong
PO Box 98580
Tsim Sha Tsui Post Office
Kowloon
Hong Kong
Tel: 3–7221634

# Characters Around the Cross

### By the Rev Tom Houston

The Cross of Jesus, leading to the Resurrection, imposes meaning upon the inherently tragic nature of life. Tom Houston, in this fascinating and often moving book, leads us through the events and emotions surrounding the Crucifixion.

Peter, Pilate, the crowds who demanded Christ's death, Mary Magdalene—experience the events with them; gain insight into their motives, their love, their grief.

'Not only do the market-places, courtrooms, streets and shrines take on a new earthly reality, but the writings of their day bear a striking relevance to our own world.'

*Today*, April, 1986

The Rev Tom Houston, formerly Executive Director of the British and Foreign Bible Society, is now President of World Vision International.

160pp                                               £1.95

# God's Mission:
# Healing the Nations

### By Dr David Burnett

God's healing: the streams of the water of life. Christians
are the messengers carrying that healing mission from
God: calming, reconciling, easing conflict. Who can ignore
such a commission from God? It is not a soft option, says
Dr Burnett, but a command we are challenged to obey.

GOD'S MISSION: HEALING THE NATIONS
explores the vision of mission throughout the ages. Dr
Burnett examines the divergences in concept and
understanding lucidly and with compassion—challenging
us to realise that mission is both a calling and a privilege
which none of us can afford to turn away from.

Discussion questions, suggested readings and an
extensive booklist are practical aids in pursuing the topic
beyond the printed page.

David Burnett is Principal of the Missionary Orientation
Centre at the WEC International headquarters at
Bulstrode in Buckinghamshire. He has served as a
missionary in India, and he and his wife, Anne, have two
children.

*Co-published with the Evangelical Missionary Alliance and
Send the Light Books.*
256pp                                                    £2.75

# Theatrecraft

### By Nigel Forde

At last a superbly written insight into the world of drama takes centre stage!

THEATRECRAFT is the perfect book to guide the aspiring drama group, while providing added insights for those more experienced in drama production. Nigel Forde, writing from 20 years' experience as a professional actor, playwright and producer, places a Christian perspective on the theory and practice of drama.

THEATRECRAFT covers acting, stagecraft, directing, writing and stage management, as well as discussing the theology of the theatre and the role of the artist. Nigel Forde writes with humour and vitality: THEATRE-CRAFT is a superbly written, clear-thinking insight into the world of drama.

Nigel Forde is a director of the Riding Lights Theatre Company in York. He is also resident poet of BBC Radio 4's 'Midweek' programme and a regular writer for the same channel's 'Start the Week'. He was a finalist in last year's Observer/Arvon International Poetry Competition.

189pp                                                    £2.25

# Ten Worshipping Churches

**Edited by Graham Kendrick**

'Worship'—the word calls forth images of people flocking
to pay honour to God, to show their love and reverence in
services as varied as the buildings that enclose them. But
what is worship? How can we enliven and enjoy our
worship and make it pleasing to God?

Graham Kendrick, well known songwriter and worship
leader, draws together ten churches of different affiliations
across Britain to discover some surprising and exciting
answers to these questions. Gone is the notion of staid,
stuffy services. Instead, old frameworks are built upon and
polished to a new lustre with experiments in drama,
unstructured or free-flowing worship, music, liturgy, and
full orchestral accompaniments!

The ten contributors to this book show an understanding
for and sensitivity to the feelings of some members of their
congregations who wish to maintain tradition, while at the
same time an open attitude towards new forms. They write
with warmth about what is happening in their churches,
charting both the joys and difficulties of worship within a
climate of change and sometimes even conflict. What
emerges is a dynamic picture of people of varied
backgrounds learning to worship together.

**A book to encourage and enlighten you!**

*Published jointly with the British Church Growth Association*
192pp                                                              £2.25

# Seconds Away!

### By Dr David Cormack

Having been given the gift of life and time, no one can misuse it more than you. SECONDS AWAY! is a course in productive living for leaders and readers of all ages. Dr Cormack will take you through 15 chapters of probing analysis, challenging you to effectively organise your time and change your lifestyle. As you assess your situation, identify your priorities, set yourself targets and 'budget' your time, each day will have infinitely more potential.

This could be one of the most important books you will ever buy—and one of the best investments.

**'Remembering that each quarter-hour was given to you by God, can you really say you made full use of it? ... a book that can change your life—as I know it is changing mine.'**
**Margaret Duggan, *Church Times***

Dr David Cormack was formerly head of Training and Organisation Development at Shell International and now serves as consultant to govenrments, businesses and charities all over the world.

183pp

£5.95 (paperback)
£12.95 (hardback)